DON'T GET ARRESTED IN SOUTH CAROLINA

A lesson of fraud, deceit, and corruption in
South Carolina law enforcement and prosecution

Erik Publishing

www.erikpublishing.com

Copyright ©2006 J. B. Simms Erik Publishing

Publisher's Cataloging-in-Publication
(Provided by Quality Books, Inc.)

Simms, J. B. (James B.)
Don't get arrested in South Carolina: the documentation
of fraud, deceit
and corruption in South Carolina law enforcement and
prosecution / J.B. Simms.
    p. cm.
"The truth regarding the investigation into the death of
Dr. Harry Sunshine, and
the secrets the police agencies and the prosecution did
not want exposed to the public." ISBN-13: 978-0-9795766-
0-7 —ISBN-10: 0-9795766-0-1
    1. Sunshine, Harry. 2. Outlaw, Charles. 3. Homicide
investigation—
South Carolina—Columbia.   4. Police corruption--
South Carolina--Columbia.
    5. Political corruption--South Carolina—Columbia.   I.
Title.

    HV6533.S6S56   2007
    364.152939097577QBI07-600160

Contents

Acknowledgments

These are the brave persons who believed in this project while others shied away from truth.

First, my son, who never discouraged the project and assisted greatly during the process. Frankly, he has never shied away from anything.

Second, Jesse Fortner, who was in contact almost daily, and assisted in more ways than you can imagine, and she was always willing to go the extra mile.

Will Moredock, Charleston, SC, author of The Banana Republic, encouraged this first project of mine and always answered my calls and questions.

My friend Margaret Gallagher, who has known of my investigative work for almost 20 years, worked sources on the West Coast for me, always had good advice, and believed in me.

Mary Dellucci, my internet guru and drummer in Charleston, had candid and important things to say. She is an angel.

My editor, Susan Snowden, my composition agent Anne Landgraf, and my cover designer Susan Miller, all put up with all my questions, repeated emails and telephone calls. You ladies were great. Thank you so much.

My friends, Ron and Meg Suich, whose combined friendship, generosity, hospitality, and faith in this project enabled me to focus and get this done. I will always be in their debt.

There are some friends who chose not to be mentioned because it would affect their professional lives. They know they are still my friends, the good guys, who have helped in their own way. Some of those were local and federal law enforcement officers, some are attorneys, some are former drug dealers. Some expressed fear for my safety. Thank you.

And to all those who kept telling me that I should not, could not, and would not write this book, I do not envy your life of fear and trepidation. You are afraid of the truth. Some are involved in the criminal enterprise outlined in this book, and live in their own secret criminality.

J.B. Simms

Introduction

Harry Sunshine was a loved and respected man. He was loved by his wife, children, family, and everyone with whom he came in contact. He was an extremely popular children's dentist and touched the lives of many people. People came from all over to bring their children to Dr. Sunshine's office. He was also a vibrant member of the Jewish community in Columbia, South Carolina. Even Leon Lott, the sheriff of Richland County, stated he was a personal friend of this tight-knit family.

Dr. Sunshine was a healthy man. He took care of himself. He rode his bicycle alone for long distances as part of his health routine, sometimes in the early morning hours. Everyone expected Dr. Sunshine to live a long and healthy life. This assumption was shattered when the media announced that Dr. Sunshine had been killed while riding the bicycle he enjoyed so much. He was killed September 30, 2000, struck by a vehicle and left to die on the side of a road.

Tshona Gaymon Outlaw and Charles Outlaw, a married black couple, were arrested and charged with involvement in the death of Dr. Harry Sunshine. Tshona Outlaw was charged with hit and run. Charles was charged with owning the vehicle which struck Dr. Sunshine. Newspapers printed their photographs and detailed stories about their identities, as well as the police account of their supposed involvement. Television accounts also showed their photographs. The South Carolina Highway Patrol, Richland County Sheriff's Department, and the South Carolina Law Enforcement Division had representatives interviewed, giving sound bites that Tshona and Charles ran away to avoid being arrested. A photograph of a wrecked car was given to the media by the authorities, stating, not alleging, that the wrecked car belonged to Charles Outlaw. An additional charge of Accessory after the Fact was placed against Charles almost a year later. This charge alleged that Charles hid information about the crime, and hid his wife from the authorities.

That is what you heard or read from the local media. The media got their information from the authorities. If you believe everything you read and hear from the media, then you have no need to read this book. If you want to live your life believing that you can trust everything you are told by someone in authority, then you won't want to read this book; it would be far too frightening for you.

This book is the true account of the investigation of the death of Dr. Sunshine, and the attempt to convict an innocent man to protect the identity of someone else, or other people. The investigation revealed information that not only implicated the law enforcement community, but also prison officials, defense attorneys, inmates and former inmates, and bank officials. It also involved missing and destroyed documents, and the filing of false affidavits.

This revelation of the inner workings of the establishment is a lesson for everyone who believed in the system, or had the nerve to challenge the system. It is also a sad revelation about the victims, both deceased and alive.

Index of Individuals

Dr. Harry Sunshine—Killed by hit and run driver at approximately 5:45 a.m. on Saturday, September 30, 2000, Columbia, SC.

Charles Outlaw—Owner of 1994 black Lexus, accused of owning the vehicle which struck Dr. Sunshine.

Tshona Gaymon Outlaw—Wife of Charles Outlaw. She was driving husband's 1994 Lexus on the morning of September 30, 2000.

J.B. Simms—Investigator hired by Charles Outlaw and the family of Tshona Gaymon.

Laura Outlaw—Mother of Charles Outlaw.

Brandi Outlaw—9-year-old child of Charles and Tshona Outlaw.

Sgt. Thomas Collins—South Carolina Highway Patrol. Arresting officer of Charles Outlaw and Tshona Gaymon who obtained the warrant for Charles Outlaw's arrest from Judge Michael Davis.

Suhail Najjar—Manager of Hi-Line Imports, Columbia, SC.

Jerry Finney—Attorney, Columbia, SC. Made initial unsolicited visit to Charles Outlaw.

Judge Ernest Finney (Ret.)—Father of Jerry Finney. Both met with Outlaw family upon Outlaw's release from jail on bail. Retired SC Supreme Court Chief Justice.

Forcina Gaymon—Mother of Tshona Gaymon Outlaw, lived in New York City.

John E. Brown—Former owner of Ampro Security, and law enforcement officer. Boyfriend of Forcina Gaymon, who is the mother of Tshona Gaymon.

K.C. Brown—Brother of John E. Brown, former employee of John E. Brown.

Carlos Parson—driver for John E. Brown.

Sandra Lambright—Sister of Forcina Gaymon, aunt of Tshona Gaymon.

Mamchu S. Jeff—Daughter of Sandra Lambright. Called Tshona Gaymon Outlaw to go to a party on the night before Dr. Sunshine was killed.

Leon Lott— Sheriff of Richland County, Columbia, SC.

Captain Jim Stewart—Officer with Richland County Sheriff's Department.

Robert D. Stewart—Chief of South Carolina Law Enforcement Division.

Judge Michael Davis—Magistrate, Richland County, SC. Signed arrest warrant at the request of and based upon testimony of Sgt. Thomas Collins.

Larry Aaron—(deceased) Owner of Aaron Body Shop.

Ray Porter—Employee of Larry Aaron, Aaron Body Shop.

James Brown—Observed Charles and Tshona Gaymon on the morning of Saturday, September 30, 2000 as they stopped and argued while en route to Hi-Line Imports. Mr. Brown also witnessed Charles reporting the damage to a police officer. Employed with temporary service.

Atlanta Auto Auction—Point of origin of 1993 Lexus and 1994 Lexus on the lot of Hi-Line Imports.

Barney Giese—Prosecutor (Solicitor) for Richland County, SC.

Johnny Gasser—Assistant Solicitor for Richland County, SC. Initially assigned to prosecute Charles Outlaw by his boss, Barney Giese.

Bill O'Neill—Investigator for the office of the Richland County Solicitor's Office.

David Pascoe—Assistant Solicitor for Richland County, SC.

Fila Jamison—Former boyfriend of Tshona Gaymon Outlaw.

Committed shooting in the apartment he shared with Tshona during a separation from Charles Outlaw.

Todd Rutherford—Attorney who represented Charles from January 2001 through August 2001.

Dennis Bolt—Attorney who represented Charles beginning August 2001 through September 2003.

Stephen Geoly—Attorney who was retained by Charles in February 2004.

Sherma Doughty—Friend of Tshona Gaymon Outlaw. Was said to have been with Tshona on the night of the death Dr. Sunshine.

Shermica Doughty—Sister of Sherma Doughty.

Chapter One

This is not a story of authorities attempting to prosecute an innocent man, or just a story of the authorities attempting to illegally coerce a false statement from a man. It is the story of a tangled conspiracy to protect the identity of a guilty man, who was described by a witness, at the cost of another man's freedom, reputation, health, money, and family. The conspiracy involved three police agencies, prosecutors, attorneys, and a former chief justice of the South Carolina Supreme Court.

Dr. Harry Sunshine was killed Saturday, September 30, 2000. He was struck and killed while riding his bicycle on Two Notch Road in Columbia, South Carolina. The time of his death was approximately 5:45 a.m. No one came forth stating they witnessed the accident. A passerby saw Dr. Sunshine and his bicycle on the side of the road. Someone just left him to die, and rendered no aid. The horror the family suffered could not be described.

On November 29, 2000, Charles Outlaw was arrested and charged with failure to report a traffic accident with damages exceeding one thousand dollars. The accident supposedly involved a vehicle which Charles purchased on September 27, 2000, a few days before the accident. Charles' wife, Tshona, had been arrested for the hit and run death of Dr. Harry Sunshine, children's dentist and prominent member of the community, on September 30, 2000.

A witness surfaced a month later after having been ignored by the authorities for weeks. The witness, Sharon Keels, just happened to recognize Dr. Sunshine's widow at the post office where Ms. Keels worked, and told Ms. Sunshine she saw a black Lexus on Two Notch Road on the morning of Dr. Sunshine's death. Ms. Keels stated a black man was in the passenger seat. She told this to the Richland County Sheriff's Department, but no one interviewed her. They could no longer ignore this witness.

The authorities used the statement of the witness to get a description of a vehicle observed in the area about the time of the death of Dr. Sunshine. But when the witness identified a black female driver and a black man in the passenger seat, it did not fit into the plans of the police or prosecution. So, they placed a petite black female into the passenger seat to replace the adult black male witnessed by the postal worker. The police were determined to (1) prosecute a driver, (2) put the driver into a different vehicle, and (3) change the identity of the passenger witnessed by the postal worker.

The authorities were also determined to use only the part of the witness's statement that they wanted to use. They used a paper dealer tag to direct them to a car dealership. The witness could not identify the driver of the car in a photo lineup; Shona's picture was one of the photos. The authorities decided not to publish that information about the witness, nor did the authorities want it published that the female driver had a black male passenger. It just did not fit their plan.

They certainly did not plan for Charles Outlaw to fight the authorities. It almost killed him.

Charles Outlaw called my office on the morning of April 30, 2001. Charles told me that he had been arrested for failing to report a traffic accident which occurred on September 30, 2000. He was very animated, talking loudly and very fast. Charles was from New York City, which explained his rapid-fire account of the events. After having conducted criminal investigations since 1981, I was aware that I would need to meet with him and get a lot more information. The initial charge was so minor that I could not understand why he was so adamant about battling the charge against him, which was a misdemeanor.

Charles told me he had talked to other private investigators and not one would touch the case. There was too much publicity. His attorney had not even scheduled a preliminary hearing for him. Charles was so frustrated.

Charles was never in the vehicle which struck Dr. Sunshine, and had no knowledge of the crime. The authorities arrested Charles, and sent him a private defense attorney. The arresting officer from the SC Highway Patrol told Charles' mother that he had sent Charles an attorney, and that Charles should listen to the attorney. The attorney who visited Charles in jail, the arresting officer, and the father of the attorney (the retired SC Supreme Court Chief Justice) tried to get Charles to sign a statement against his wife. Charles refused. A prosecutor took Charles into his office with no defense attorney present, and tried to convince Charles to take a plea. Charles refused. Charles was not going to be intimidated by unscrupulous people, and did not know the reason for all the coverup and lies. Charles would not do the illegal things the authorities told him to do, so they added an additional charge of hit and run against him.

The story began on the evening of Friday, September 29, 2000.

Charles 'wife, Tshona, began receiving repeated telephone calls from her cousin, Mamchu. Mamchu wanted Tshona to go with her to a huge social function in Columbia. Jermaine O'Neal, a local high school basketball player and now a professional player, had just signed a contract with the Indiana Pacers of the National Basketball Association. The celebration was at the Sheraton Hotel. Tshona borrowed Charles' 1994 Lexus and dropped her daughter off with her aunt Debra. That night would change the lives of many people.

When Charles got up the next morning, Tshona was home. Charles went outside and found a horizontal scrape on the bumper of his car. The striations on the bumper were similar to scraping against a concrete barrier or wall. The fog light was intact but diagonally cracked. The headlight was intact. The fender was not bent. The hood was not bent. The windshield was not cracked. The door post on the passenger side was not damaged. If that vehicle had struck a pedestrian or a person on a bicycle, most or all those areas would be damaged. That vehicle had struck no one. But Charles was to find out later that his vehicle would be implicated by the authorities.

Tshona told Charles that she scraped a barrier at the Sheraton Hotel. It was not until later that I found out that was probably true. It would be sometime later that Charles and I would know for sure that his car was not involved in the death of Dr. Sunshine.

Charles told me that the television stations showed pictures of a car that was said to have been involved in the death of Dr. Sunshine. That vehicle was crashed on the passenger side. So, the pictures of the vehicle on the news reports were not of Charles' vehicle. The more I listened to Charles the more I knew that there were big issues in the case.

Charles' photograph had been shown on the television news as theowner of the vehicle which killed Dr. Sunshine. Charles could not go anywhere without people pointing at him and saying he was involved in the death of the doctor. Law enforcement officers were being interviewed on television naming Charles as the driver. Charles knew he was far away from the accident when it happened, and he knew nothing about the accident. Charles was right; there was a feeding frenzy with respect to media coverage.

After meeting with Charles in my office, I drove to Charles' house, located in the southern part of Columbia. He lived with his mother in a black neighborhood. The homes were modest brick homes, and most of the yards were well kept. There were kids always playing in the street. A well-known drug area was a few blocks away, but the area was quiet.

I was going to talk with Laura, Charles' mother. Ms. Laura Outlaw was a middle aged black woman. Laura was very articulate, and a very nice woman. She was a Jehovah's Witness by faith. She was very knowledgeable about interaction with crime and the police, having retired as a teacher in New York City. After retiring from teaching, Laura returned to Columbia a few years before the death of Dr. Sunshine.

While living in New York City, Charles lived with Laura, where Charles met Tshona. Tshona and Charles lived separately until they were married. Tshona gave birth to a child, and Charles raised the child as his own, most of the time in his mother's home. The child was nine years old when Dr. Sunshine was killed. Her name was Brandi.

Tshona was not an attentive mother; Charles and Laura raised Brandi. Laura told me that Tshona would disappear and not come back for hours. There were many times when Tshona would not have food for Brandi, so Charles and Laura had to feed the child when Tshona would drop the child off.

When Laura moved back to South Carolina, Charles, Tshona, and Brandi came with her. Charles and Tshona got their own apartment, but Tshona continued to drop Brandi off with Laura when Charles was working and Tshona wanted to go out. Just before they returned to South Carolina, Tshona announced to Charles that Brandi was not his biological child; the man identified as the father was now residing in Atlanta. Charles kept raising Brandi as his own, and Laura, heartbroken as she was, continued to be the attentive grandmother.

After Charles and Tshona were arrested, the biological father took Brandi to Atlanta and filed for custody against Tshona, claiming he was the biological father. No DNA test was ever conducted to prove it, and Charles did not have the money to fight the allegation. Laura had lost Brandi and her daughter-in-law, and her son had been accused of something he did not do: being involved in the death of Harry Sunshine.

Before Tshona married Charles, Tshona had been living with her mother, Forcina Gaymon, on the lower west side of Manhattan. When Tshona met Charles, Laura met Forcina and they realized that they both had relatives and ties to South Carolina. That was no surprise. Many blacks went north for work due to prejudice in the South.

While Laura and Forcina were living in New York, Laura learned from Forcina that she had a boyfriend who lived in South Carolina. Forcina told Laura that the boyfriend used to be a police officer, and owned a big security company in Columbia. The boyfriend was also married. Laura asked Forcina why Forcina would want to be involved with a married man. Forcina told Laura that the boyfriend "buys her things." Charles had been told by Tshona that Forcina had a cocaine problem. Forcina could not afford to buy the cocaine she was using, so Forcina had her "friend buy her things."

Laura continued, telling me that she was upset that Charles' attorney, Todd Rutherford, was not helping Charles, her son. She was upset that the police had sent the lawyer they chose to see Charles while Charles was in jail, and that the father of that attorney, the retired Supreme Court Chief Justice, tried to get Charles to give a false statement claiming that Tshona told Charles she had struck Dr. Sunshine with Charles' vehicle. Laura was present with another witness when the retired chief justice made the statement. Laura wondered why these people were doing all these unscrupulous things to her and to Charles. Laura and Charles had never hurt anyone.

Before Charles was arrested, an agent named Tad Reed from the South Carolina Law Enforcement Division came into her house asking questions about Charles and Tshona, Charles' car, and the death of Dr. Sunshine. Laura told Agent Reed that Tshona had never mentioned the accident, and that Charles and Tshona were out of town visiting Tshona's family for Thanksgiving. Laura told Agent Reed that she had been in touch with Charles and Tshona and that neither had stated they had any knowledge of the crime; they did not understand why they were being targeted as suspects in the death of Dr. Sunshine.

Agent Reed then asked Laura for her Social Security number. Laura thought that was an odd request. Agent Reed became infuriated because Laura could not tell him exactly where Charles was. Agent Reed kept firing questions at Laura. Laura asked why Reed would need her Social Security number, but Reed gave no explanation. Reed demanded the number. Laura refused. Reed then pulled his coat jacket back away from his pants, exposing his firearm. Reed placed his hand on his firearm and told her, "I am not going to ask you again." Laura got scared. She gave him her Social Security number as well as Charles' cell phone number, which Reed demanded. Welcome to the South Carolina criminal justice system.

I told Laura that any police officer could get her Social Security number from multiple databases available to them. I subscribed to databases that would give the information within seconds. Laura thought, "Here I am, a middle-aged black woman living in South Carolina, and a white SLED agent threatens me with his gun, and he can do anything he wants to me. Is he going to arrest me?"

Laura was later told by SC Highway Patrol Officer Thomas Collins that there was a warrant for the arrest of Charles and Tshona, and that Charles' car hit Dr. Sunshine. Laura wondered why they had a warrant when the police had not even seen his car. She had seen the car. That car had struck no one.

Now Laura knew they would do whatever they wanted, and get away with it.

J.B. Simms

Arrest Warrant

Newspaper Clippings of Arrest

Husband's bond reduced in hit-and-run

Wife remains charged with reckless homicide in Dr. Harry Sunshine's death in bicycle accident

Sunday, Dec. 3, 2000

FROM PAGE ONE / NATION

HUSBAND
FROM PAGE A1

Chapter Two

Charles was sitting with Laura and me at their home, he told me the story of coming to South Carolina with Tshona and being introduced to Forcina's boyfriend. Charles and Tshona went to Summerton, South Carolina to a mobile home, which the boyfriend was said to have purchased for Forcina. Forcina's mother had a home in that town.

Charles was introduced to the boyfriend. His name was John Brown.

John Brown, a former officer with the SC Highway Patrol, was assigned to a driving detail, driving former governor John West. After leaving the SC Highway Patrol, Brown was named as the head of a company called Ampro. Ampro was a security firm, and was getting minority contracts with the government, and since Brown was a black man, he was placed as owner of the company. Truth was that Governor West was backing the company. Governor West had all the contacts and saw a use for Brown. Brown had no business background.

Charles told me that the warrant for his arrest had a tag number written on the warrant. Charles purchased the 1994 Lexus on September 27, 2000, and was given a paper tag with no number on it. When Charles was arrested on November 29, 2000 during the Thanksgiving holiday at Tshona's family's house in Atlanta, the vehicle still had the paper tag. That was one of the many fabrications the police used to implicate Charles in the crime. The permanent tag had never been received by Charles.

Forcina Gaymon, Tshona's mother, was also at the Thanksgiving family gathering, having traveled to Atlanta from her home in New York City. Charles and Tshona traveled to Atlanta from Columbia, where they were living in an apartment.

Charles' job at the time of the accident was detailing cars at a major automobile dealership in Columbia. He knew and could identify vehicles. He knew that the vehicle shown on television was not his car. My main concern was defending Charles against the charges, not solving the crime. But, as time went on, we would prove that Charles

was telling the truth, and that the police had a reason to lie.

Charles told me that during the week after he noticed the scrape on his bumper, he and Tshona went to the insurance company to place a claim on his insurance policy. The vehicle was inspected by Jimmy Winders at the insurance company. Mr. Winders took photographs of the vehicle, inspected the vehicle, and told Charles he was submitting a claim to his insurance company.

Now was the time for Charles and me to go see Mr. Winders. Charles and I left Charles' house and went to Leon Jones Insurance

Company. Upon arriving, Charles and I talked to Mr. Winders. Mr. Winders stated that he took the photographs of Charles' 1994 Lexus with a digital camera and that there were no originals of the photos. Mr. Winders stated he had erased the photo card when the card became full. Charles asked Mr. Winders for a copy of the report of damage that he sent to the insurance carrier in order to have the claim processed. Mr. Winders told us that the report would have to be subpoenaed. Mr. Winders would not give us a copy of the document, even though the policy was in Charles' name. We did not know if that was business as usual, but our hands were tied.

I asked Mr. Winders about the damage to Charles' car, which he inspected. Mr. Winders told me that the car had white scratches but had no evidence of impact, as in an accident. There were no missing parts and no broken lights.

Tshona told him that she scraped the car on a concrete barrier. Mr. Winders did not question that to me.

It did not make sense that Charles would not be entitled to copies of his paperwork, and that Mr. Winders' used the word "subpoena" in order for Charles to get a copy of his own records. That was not business as usual. Who told Mr. Winders not to give the documents to Charles? My office was located less than two minutes from Leon Jones Insurance Company, so Charles and I decided to go back to my office and talk. Jimmy was said to be part owner of the company.

Charles was upset, and rightfully so. He was very frustrated because he had no information concerning the events of the evening or of the accident, and yet he was being accused of knowing everything. If Tshona had information about that night, she did not share it with Charles.

He was also frustrated that Mr. Winders would not give him a copy of his own file. Dr. Sunshine's death was a high-profile tragedy and was all over the news. Charles knew that Mr. Winders was aware of the death of Dr. Sunshine, and he knew that the vehicle which Mr. Winders inspected was not the car that killed Dr. Sunshine. That written information would be crucial. It would not hurt Mr. Winders to give it up. Mr. Winders was apparently being controlled.

It became clear from early on that we would have to fight the establishment.

Charles told me that his wife, Tshona, had said she was with Sherma Doughty on the night of the accident. Tshona did not realize that Charles knew she had received many calls from her cousin Mamchu before going to the party. So, if she left to meet Mamchu, and dropped her child off with her aunt Debra, what happened between Tshona and Mamchu that night?

As we sat in my office Charles and I continued to talk. Charles had Sherma's telephone number. I called the number, put Sherma on the speaker phone, and we began talking. I told Charles just to listen in the beginning, but I did not disguise to Sherma the fact that Charles was in the room.

Sherma Doughty had never spoken to me before that day, but she was very open and informative. She stated that on the night before the accident she had gone to the party at the Sheraton but did not see Tshona. Sherma did not see Tshona until around 1:00 a.m. on Saturday morning at a club called Fantasy Island. Charles did not know that Tshona had gone to Fantasy Island that night, and the look on his face told me that was the first time he had heard about it.

Fantasy Island was a black strip club. It was known for rampant drug activity and prostitution. What was the reason for Tshona to be there? Who told her to go to there after the party at the Sheraton?

Sherma told us that she had gone to the party at the Sheraton with her sister Shermica and their cousin, who was visiting from out of town. Sherma saw Tshona at approximately 1:00 a.m. at Fantasy Island, and when the club closed at around 3:00 a.m. all four girls decided to go to another club. Sherma got into the 1994 Lexus with Tshona. Sherma told me that she was very drunk when she got into the car with Tshona. Shermica drove her own car and her cousin was the passenger in Shermica's car. Both cars left Fantasy Island soon after 3:00 a.m.

About five minutes later, as the two cars traveled up Two Notch Road, approaching Fontaine Road, Shermica pulled alongside Tshona's vehicle. Sherma was lying on the console of Tshona's car, barely able to hold her head up. Shermica rolled down her window and told Tshona and Sherma that she had to go to work at Wal-Mart in a few hours and had decided not to go to the other club. Tshona then turned left toward Fontaine Road. Shermica went in the opposite direction.

There was little traffic on the road. The time was just after 3:00 a.m. Tshona had turned left from Two Notch Road onto Fontaine Road. She traveled about a half mile, turned right onto Interstate 277, which would lead her to Interstate 20, which circumvented the north part of Columbia. Upon reaching Interstate 20, Tshona could turn west and go to the club. But, as Tshona reached Interstate-277, Sherma stated she began to feel really sick, and there was no way she would be able to go to a club. Sherma told Tshona to take her home. Home for Sherma was in the opposite direction from the club where they were going.

Sherma told Charles and me that the route Tshona would take to get to Sherma's apartment would have been to travel east on Interstate 20 until she reached the Clemson Road exit, a distance of about eight miles. Tshona would exit Interstate 20 onto Clemson Road, turn left onto Clemson Road, then turn left onto Sparkleberry Road. Sherma lived in an apartment on Sparkleberry Road, directly across from Spring Valley High School.

I knew that area. There was no reason for Tshona to have traveled north on Two Notch Road in order to take Sherma home. The girls were going to go to the club, and they had already driven onto Interstate

277. When Sherma decided she was too sick to go to the club, Tshona certainly would not have backed up and retraced her steps to go back to Two Notch Road. There were fewer police on the interstate than on Two Notch Road, and no traffic lights. As she approached the stop sign at the Clemson Road exit, Tshona knew she had to turn left. That would put her five minutes or less from Sherma's apartment. As Tshona would turn left, a high concrete curb would be on her right. I did not know until I looked at the

curb if it was high enough to scrape the fender, but there was paint from other cars on the curb. The fender on the Lexus was very low. (See Appendix map)

Sherma said that just before they arrived at the apartment, Sherma felt the car scrape something. Tshona and Sherma got out of the car, looked at the car, and found nothing wrong with the car. Nothing was broken; no glass, metal, or anything that looked like she had hit anything that would have damaged the car. The two continued to Sherma's apartment. Sherma got out of the car, and before going into the apartment, both she and Tshona looked at the car again. The air dam under the car was hanging down. When Sherma said that, Charles jumped in and told us that the air dam was hanging down when he bought the car. The dealer, Hi-Line Imports, was supposed to fix it sometime after the sale. It was never fixed. Some of the screws were missing, and Suhail, the manager, told Charles he would put new screws in to hold up the air dam.

Sherma continued by saying that after Charles and Tshona had been arrested in Atlanta, three police officers came to her apartment during the evening, wanting to come in and interview her. One was a Richland County Sheriff's Deputy, and the other two were plainclothes detectives. Sherma was scared and surprised that three cops would come into her home at that late hour to get a statement from her. She told them that she was intoxicated and went home after leaving the club. Sherma said that the club was closing at 3:00 a.m., and that she would have been home no later than 3:30 a.m. Dr. Sunshine was killed at approximately 5:45 a.m.

Sherma further told us that after checking the vehicle on the way home, and at the apartment, and after noticing no real damage to the car (she could not see the horizontal scrape, or just did not notice it by the streetlight) Tshona's demeanor had not changed. Tshona did not appear to have any anxiety. The possibility of the car having hit someone or an animal did not cross either of their minds. Finally, Sherma told me she would be glad to give me a statement.

Once Sherma was off the phone, Charles vented. He restated that when he bought the 1994 Lexus, it had scratches on the passenger fender and the air dam was hanging down. To compound the problem for the police, the scrape on the bumper did not match the crime scene because Dr. Sunshine was struck on the open road, with wide grassy shoulders, and no concrete anywhere in the area. It was clear to me that Tshona could not have struck Dr. Sunshine on Two Notch Road in Charles' car.

Charles was very angry to learn that Tshona had gone to Fantasy Island. He knew that Fantasy Island was a black strip club and he did not know why Tshona would be there. It became clear that there were parts of the evening that Tshona did not reveal to Charles.

Charles told me that he had heard that John Brown, Forcina's boyfriend, was out that night. John Brown's brother, K.C. Brown, was also said to be out at the party at the Sheraton. Charles told me that people were coming up to Charles telling him things.

I knew that John Brown lived in the Wildewood subdivision which was near the location of the death of Dr. Sunshine. When Ampro was going bankrupt and Johnny Brown's friend and employee Duane Everett was trying to help John Brown sell the company, it was big news. Here was a black man who had made a lot of money as a minority entrepreneur, and the company was in financial ruin. The local newspapers published stories about the downfall of Ampro, the escapades of Mr. Brown with a woman from Atlanta, and the fact that Mr. Brown had wrecked a vehicle on the property of a fellow resident of the Wildewood subdivision. All of this was no secret.

Laura also had heard that there was a connection between John Brown and Dr. Sunshine's death. Laura's cousin had run a towing service, and had died a brief time after Charles was arrested in November 2000. Her cousin's nickname was Happy Daddy, and "Happy" had run a towing service for many years. I remembered investigating traffic accidents in 1986 and having to go take photographs of vehicles at Happy's garage.

According to Laura, Happy went on to say that soon after Dr. Sunshine's death John Brown's wife's car broke down and Happy had to tow the car. Ms. Brown, who was employed at that time with the SC Law Enforcement Division, told Happy that she did not have a car to drive. Happy told her that she should use the black Lexus that he had seen John driving. Ms. Brown got real loud and mad at Happy; she denied that John ever drove a black Lexus. Happy told Laura that he knew better, and was amused at Ms. Brown.

Happy knew everybody in the black community. He was a successful businessman, and was respected in that community. When Charles got arrested, Laura went to Happy to ask for help pay the bond to get Charles out of jail. During the time that Happy was putting up the money, Happy told Laura that John Brown was involved in the death of Dr. Sunshine. To quote Laura, Happy told Laura that John Brown was a "dirty nigger." Laura told me that those were the exact words Happy used.

I told Charles I knew a black man who was a licensed private investigator. The man had done a little work for me years ago and he acted like he knew everybody who was anybody. I had come to find out that he really was not respected for his investigative skills or intellect and he would come around my office from time to time. I knew he was a big-name dropper, but the people who professionally associated with him were those in the black community. I suggested we pay him a visit.

Charles and I went to meet the man at a fast food restaurant. He told us that he knew all the players, the members of the Brown family, and acted as if he had information that would help Charles find out what happened on the night Dr. Sunshine was killed. He was really animated, and told us he could find out all sorts of things. He told us that he knew all these people and he had heard stuff on the street, but he really was not saying anything of value. The guy wanted Charles to retain him or associate himself with me on the case. Plus, he wanted a lot of money from Charles.

We were not interested in hiring him. He was personable and a nice fellow, but he could not withstand the scrutiny that the case would bring on everyone involved. We did not want to tell him much because we did not know where his loyalty was placed. His role was to be an informant and not to be involved in any part of the investigation, so I just let him fade away.

I told Charles that my involvement was out in the open now. The black private investigator was going to get on the phone and meet some people to tell them what we were doing. The case would implicate some powerful people, and we knew it.

In the following days, I got more background information from Charles. Charles and Laura were sure that the vehicle shown on television was not Charles' car. Charles kept saying that there was a similar car out there on that night.

Charles was arrested in Atlanta during Thanksgiving holidays 2000 and he was transported to Columbia. After getting out of jail on bail in early December 2000, Charles went back to Hi-Line Imports to talk to Suhail Najjar, who had sold Charles his 1994 Lexus. The date of the visit was

December 23, 2000. When Charles bought the car, Suhail told Charles that he would pay to have the scratches on the fender touched up, and have the drooping air dam reattached.

Upon arriving at Hi-Line Imports on December 23, 2000, Charles saw a 1993 Lexus. It was black, just like Charles' car. The 1993 Lexus was backed up to a fence and it was heavily damaged. The passenger side fender was crushed, the headlight and fog light assembly was broken, the hood was bent, and the door post was dented. The windshield was broken on the passenger side as well.

Charles was naïve to think he would be getting his car back soon (the police had impounded his 1994 Lexus after transporting it from Atlanta). Charles also wanted his tags. He asked Suhail for the license tags which were to be sent to Suhail from the SC Highway Department.

Suhail told Charles that Charles still owed money for the down payment, a claim which Charles denied. It was later determined that Hi-Line Imports filled out two bills of sale for two different amounts. The lending institution, First Citizens Bank, had a bill of sale which was different from the one Charles had, and the sale price was different. When I brought it to the attention of the bank, nothing was done. It was also brought to the attention of the SC Highway Department, car dealer division. Again, nothing was done.

Charles found Suhail on the lot and asked him about the wrecked 1993 Lexus. Suhail told Charles that when the police came to his lot after the accident they saw the 1993 Lexus. They told Suhail that the witness had given a statement about a black Lexus having been seen in the vicinity of the crime, and the vehicle having a Hi-Line Imports paper tag. Suhail told Charles that the police took pictures of the 1993 Lexus, and Suhail did not say much about the car after that.

Now Hi-Line Imports had involved First Citizens Bank. Their involvement later became more heinous.

Charles wanted me to accompany him to see Suhail. It was as if Charles thought he was telling me something I did not believe, but the cover-up was growing and I wanted to see it for myself. He wanted to see if the 1993 Lexus was still there. Charles used to detail cars for a living and could recognize automobiles by make and model much better than I could.

When we got to Hi-Line Imports, Charles saw the 1993 Lexus immediately. It had been repaired and painted. We approached the car and a salesman came up to us. His name was Anthony Kelly. Anthony told us he had been told that the car, the 1993 black Lexus, had been loaned out by Hi-Line Imports but he did not know when. Anthony told us that Hi-Line Imports regularly loaned/leased the cars on their car lot for various periods of time. We confirmed that the 1993 black Lexus had been on the lot for a long time and that Anthony was now buying the car from the owner of the car lot, Suhail. Suhail had not told Anthony that the 1993 Lexus had been wrecked. Suhail was not on the lot at the time, so Charles told me that we needed to come back.

It was time to go look at Charles' car. Charles had told me that the attorney he retained, Todd Rutherford, advised Charles that he could not inspect his 1994 Lexus. The car was off limits to Charles.

Who did Rutherford think he was dealing with? The car belonged to Charles, and the defense had every right to inspect the vehicle. Rutherford was trying to keep Charles from his own car. I had never heard of an attorney not wanting the client to know information that would help exonerate him.

When Charles told me that Rutherford said that Charles would not be able to inspect his own car, I questioned that. Charles then related that Rutherford had been his attorney for the past five months and Charles had not even been given a preliminary hearing. So, Rutherford did not want Charles to see his car, and would not schedule him a preliminary hearing. Rutherford was implying to Charles that only the prosecution would have access to evidence. Charles told me he did not trust Rutherford, but that he did not know where to turn.

According to Charles, Rutherford had told Charles that he knew that Tshona did not kill Dr. Sunshine. Charles told me that Rutherford offered to get the charges dropped and insure that Tshona would be protected, for thirty thousand dollars. Laura and Charles both heard Rutherford make that offer over the telephone.

Charles had hired Rutherford because Rutherford was black. Charles thought Rutherford would look out for a fellow black man. That was a very common mindset among blacks in the South. Charles later found out that Rutherford was not to be trusted, and was not in Charles' corner.

Charles told me that his car was at the SC Highway Patrol impound located near the SC Highway Patrol headquarters on Bluff Road, on the south side of Columbia. I told Charles that we were going to go see his car and photograph his car regardless of what Rutherford said.

We went down to Bluff Road where the car was impounded. After speaking with a highway patrol officer at the headquarters building we were directed to the impound building. We walked to the building which was pointed out to us and Officer Maggertt met us at the door. I was familiar with Maggertt's name on reports of major traffic accident investigations I had conducted, but I did not know if he would remember my name.

He seemed familiar with me when I told him my name, and invited us into the building.

To our right was a car under a blue tarp. Charles and I peeled the tarp off the car from front to back and were amazed at what we first saw. Investigators had taken a sharp object and scraped paint samples off the hood, fender, and door post. On the majority of the scrapes were yellow Post-It® stickers, and they were placed on the vehicle with numbers written on the stickers.

Charles was outraged. "They have ruined my car. It didn't look like this when they got my car."

I took photographs of the car, bringing attention to the Post-It® stickers. There were a couple of long scrapes on the passenger side fender which Charles told me were on the car when he bought it. That was confirmed later from two statements from two people who test drove the car before Charles bought it. The police did not know about the people who test drove the car. We were waiting to use them as witnesses for the defense, and I could not wait to see the faces of the authorities when they testified on behalf of Charles.

I got on my back to look under the car; Charles crawled under with me. Then he yelled, "This shit is new. They put new screws in my car." What he was referring to was the fact that a number of bright shiny screws were found screwed into the underside of the car, holding up the lower air dam (gravel pan), which Charles had told me was hanging down when he bought the car. It was also confirmed by the people who had test driven the car that the air dam had been hanging down.

Charles had been telling the truth. It was not that I did not believe him, but when allegations and suppositions were confirmed and proven, I had more faith in my case and my client.

Another alteration or missing piece was found. The fog lamp had been removed. The wires had been cut, and a hole remained where the fog lamp had been removed. The fact that the fog lamp was missing was not a big issue, except when you consider that the 1993 Lexus had been repaired and that the fog lamp assembly for the 1994 and 1993 were interchangeable.

Who were the criminals now? The authorities tampered with the evidence. Charles' vehicle had been clearly altered while in police custody. In addition, the persons who were aware of the tampering and of the false statement made to obtain the warrant were accomplices. It was conspiracy. Someone had to buy the screws. Someone had to screw in the screws. Someone crawled on their back and tampered with the evidence in a death case.

The story got worse sooner than we expected. Later that same afternoon Charles and I went back to Hi-Line Imports. The black 1993 Lexus was not on the lot. While we walked around the lot we found Suhail. I had changed into some very dressed down clothes, knowing that Suhail was not supposed to know my involvement. I was posing as one of Charles' friends, observing and saying very little. That was difficult for me; I had to count on Charles to ask the right questions, and ask other questions based upon answers he got. Charles and I had talked and he knew what we needed.

As we walked inside, Charles started talking to Suhail about his car and the tag problem. Suhail said that Charles still owed him money. Both Suhail and Charles each wanted something; each was "chatting up" the other. Charles disputed owing any money, but did not want to alienate Suhail because he had information we needed. We walked down the hall to the left of the common area inside the main entrance to the office, and entered an office on the left. Suhail sat behind a desk having a computer screen on the desk. Charles and I sat in the two chairs available directly across the small desk from Suhail.

The computer screen was on the right side of Suhail. Charles and I sat facing Suhail, and the computer screen was on our left. Both Charles and I could see the computer screen.

Charles started asking Suhail about the 1993 Lexus he had seen on December 23, 2000. That was less than six months before the date we were in Suhail's office. Suhail told Charles that the police got his records of the sale of the 1994 Lexus after the witness observed a black car with a Hi-Line paper tag on the date of the accident. Charles asked Suhail if the police saw the black 1993 Lexus during their visit. Suhail replied that when the police came to his lot, which we found out later was on October 20, 2000, the police did see the wrecked black 1993 Lexus, and took pictures of the vehicle. Charles told Suhail that he had seen the car on the previous day, and that it had been painted and repaired. Suhail acknowledged that was true.

That was when the additional drama was exposed. Suhail then punched up on the computer the repair record for the 1993 Lexus in question. I think Suhail was just showing off his program on the computer but he had no idea he was implicating himself as an accessory in the cover-up in a death case. Suhail showed us the repairs which had been done on the car: a new fender for the passenger side, hood, headlight, fog lamp, as well as the housing for both the headlamp and the fog light. Bingo.

Suhail Najjar appeared to be from India or Pakistan. His wife was in the building with him when Charles and I heard him admit to having the 1993 Lexus repaired. Suhail has a family here in the United States. Suhail was someone's pigeon, and so was Sgt. Collins.

Suhail told us that when he bought the car from the auction the car was wrecked. I knew that could not be true. The car had thousands of dollars of damage and no dealer would buy a car in that condition. I would later prove that the 1993 Lexus was not wrecked when it left the auction.

Charles was talking to Suhail about the charges against him. Suhail agreed to testify to the following things: (1) Suhail stated that the damage to Charles' car was less than a thousand dollars; (2) Suhail never gave Charles the license plates, negating the information on the warrant; (3) Sgt. Collins and others inspected and photographed the wrecked 1993 Lexus on October 20, 2000; and (4) the fog lamp lens on the 1993 Lexus was cracked, not broken out or missing.

Anthony Kelly had told us that Hi-Line Imports loaned out their cars from time to time. Now I was going to prove it.

Charles told me that when he bought the 1994 Lexus he found two pieces of paper in the trunk of the car. One was a parking ticket, number 50245300, dated August 29, 2000. That was a month before Charles bought the car. The parking ticket was issued at South Carolina State University, a predominantly black school. The location of the school was Orangeburg, approximately forty-five miles from Hi-Line Imports' lot on Main Street in Columbia. The ticket was issued at the Bethea lot, adjacent to a dormitory. A student was murdered at that dormitory a few weeks after the ticket was issued.

I contacted the chief of security, Chief White. Chief White told me he voided the ticket on January 9, 2001, three months after the death of Dr. Sunshine. I knew that there was no reason to void a parking ticket, especially on a school campus. If a car had unpaid parking tickets, the car would be towed if it was recognized on campus. Students regularly get parking tickets, and the police get their cars. The vehicle identification number was on the ticket, and the correct owner's name should have been listed. The car was not in Charles' name at the time the ticket was written. The vehicle identification number was in the name of Hi-Line Imports before it was sold to Charles. The tag on the car would have been the paper tag, reading "Hi-Line Imports." Chief White decided to let it go, even though a car from 45 miles away was being given a parking ticket in the immediate vicinity of a murder that took place weeks later.

The South Carolina Law Enforcement Division (SLED) was assigned the case. I spoke to the agent in charge of the homicide investigation a number of times. Nothing was being done. I gave him the information about the vehicle from Hi-Line Imports being at the scene. The officer from SLED told me he never intended to investigate Hi-Line Imports to see who was driving that vehicle on the night of the traffic ticket, or what business that person had at a black college at night. Now SLED was involved, but not actively.

Years later, it was learned that the parking ticket was in the name of Charles Outlaw, and had a tag number. Charles bought that car a month after the ticket was given. What was someone from Hi-Line Imports doing taking that car forty-five miles away to a college dormitory? The SLED agent assigned to the case never got back to me to advise who was driving that car to a black college dormitory and known drug area. Why was the ticket in the name of Charles Outlaw, and who told the chief to dismiss the ticket?

I met with Charles at my office the day after Suhail showed Charles and me the repairs that were made on the 1993 Lexus. I told Charles that we needed to get some identification from the car. On the afternoon of May 3, 2000, at 1:20 p.m., Charles and I went back to Hi-Line Imports. The sun was high and very bright. When we arrived, Charles approached Anthony Kelly in order to get him away from the 1993 Lexus. Anthony told Charles he was told that someone traded the wrecked 1993 Lexus for an Acura. That conflicted with what Suhail had already told us: that the wrecked 1993 Lexus "was bought from an auction and was wrecked when it arrived." Suhail lied to us and to Anthony. So why did he lie?

I went over to the 1993 Lexus while Charles was talking to Anthony. I was trying to see the vehicle identification number through the glass. When I looked for the number, the glare was so bad that I had to shield the sun with my notepad. I wrote down the vehicle identification number. The number was JT8J847E9P0035717.

Charles and I left. It was hot out there, and I was anxious to see if I wrote the number down correctly. With the sun bearing down, and trying to be inconspicuous, I was trying to concentrate.

I took the information to the Jim Hudson Lexus dealership in Columbia. There I met Bobbi Brazell. Bobbi checked all the records to see if the 1993 Lexus had been repaired at the dealership. It had not been repaired at Jim Hudson Lexus, nor did they have any record of any orders for parts matching the parts damaged on the 1993 vehicle since Dr. Sunshine's death.

Bobbi was a gem. She was very intelligent and thorough. I told her what the case was about, and she was interested in helping.

I spent the next day calling car parts businesses to see if Hi-Line Imports had purchased any parts for a 1993 Lexus. There was no record of the vehicle having been repaired locally.

So, Suhail had the 1993 Lexus repair privately. SLED and Sgt. Collins did not pursue the damaged 1993 Lexus, even though they saw the vehicle and were there when it was photographed.

The next step was to obtain a vehicle history of the 1993 Lexus from the SC Highway Department. I found no record of the vehicle ever having been in an automobile accident.

I was later able to prove that the vehicle was sold to Hi-Line Imports from an auction in Atlanta, and the vehicle was not wrecked. The 1993 Lexus had been wrecked in South Carolina, and Suhail acknowledged that the wrecked vehicle, regardless of where it was wrecked, was photographed by law enforcement agents, specifically the SC Highway Patrol.

Charles was arrested on the charge of failure to report a traffic accident having property damage in excess of one thousand dollars. Why was Suhail not arrested and charged the same as Charles? Even if Suhail was not driving the car when it was damaged, Suhail had to have lied to the SC Highway Patrol, the Richland County Sheriff's Department, and the SC Law Enforcement Division when they went to Hi-Line Motors. The wrecked 1993 Lexus was a black Lexus as described by the witness, the ever-so-observant and intelligent black female postal worker. The police left Hi-Line Imports telling the media that the only black Lexus sold by Hi-Line Imports was the one sold to Charles Outlaw. "Sold" was the key word.

Suhail should have been in jail as Charles was. They should have charged Suhail with the same crime which Charles was charged. There was no record that Suhail ever filed an insurance claim, filed an accident report, or even had the car repaired locally. They left Suhail alone. He became their boy. Everybody had something to hide. People became scared, and cowards were being exposed. Many civil servants witnessed and participated in the cover-up and no one exposed it.

Statement of Sharon Keels

SOUTH CAROLINA DEPARTMENT OF PUBLIC SAFETY
SOUTH CAROLINA HIGHWAY PATROL
AFFIDAVIT

STATE OF SOUTH CAROLINA
COUNTY OF Richland

PERSONALLY appeared before me Sharon D Keels who states:

My name is Sharon D Keels . I reside at 485 White Ford Way

in Lexington . SC . 736-2262 . PER-2152

Date of Birth 2-14-68 . Social Security Number 258-21-6565

I have 12+ years of education, and I can/cannot read and write. This statement is given on November 1 , 19 2000 at 6:30 am/pm in the presence of L/CPL R.K. Hughes who has officially identified himself as a member of the SOUTH CAROLINA HIGHWAY PATROL.

On September 30, 2000 at approximately 5:30 am I was on my way to work. I exited 430 at Two Notch Road while stopped at the red light, I noticed a Black lexus to my left. When the light changed to green, I noticed that the driver of the lexus was coming over into my lane. I immediately stayed behind the vehicle and in the right hand lane. While heading north on two notch road, I noticed that the driver of the lexus was driving between both lanes. After being stopped by the red light near the red restaurant, I was closely behind the car. It was being driven by a black female who look to be approximately 25-35 years old. She had a black male passenger who appeared to be asleep. When the light changed to green, I allowed the lexus to go ahead of me. The four door did not have a South Carolina tag. It had a tag that said HI-Lites Motors. The lexus continued north on two notch road still driving between both lanes. I turned left at the Burger King to two notch and the lexus continued on down two notch road. The lexus had chrome rims. I believe the tag on this car was Hi-Lite Motors, but I am not positively sure. The tag had a dark background with light letters. SK

_____ S.K.

_____ R.K.H.

Sharon D. Keels
Affiant/Signature

Page number ONE of Two pages

Chapter Three

Now the case was taking up almost all my time. There were so many issues, and I knew that I had to be prepared to answer any question and debate any issue with respect to the case. I knew that the defense attorney was not working for Charles; he was doing a favor for his former employer, the prosecutor, by not scheduling a preliminary hearing or demanding to see documents from the prosecutor's file.

The day after Charles and I got back from getting the information on the black 1993 Lexus, Charles came to my office. He was quite upset with all that was going on. He was upset at his attorney, the police, the prosecutor, Suhail, and the cover-up. I told Charles that we had nothing to lose by going directly to his arresting officer, Sgt. Tom Collins, to see what he had to say.

We left my office and went directly to the headquarters of the SC Highway Patrol. It was mid-afternoon. We asked for Sgt. Collins, and when he appeared he led us into a small room that must have been his office. On the wall behind Sgt. Collins' desk was a picture of Charles Outlaw. I guess Sgt. Collins was a bit focused on his target, Charles Outlaw. Obsessed is a better word.

We sat across the small desk from Sgt. Collins. A credenza was behind Sgt. Collins. On the floor, next to his right foot was a large cardboard box. The word "Sunshine" was on the box. The box was the file for the case involving the death of Dr. Sunshine. Collins did not know when we were coming to see him but I had informed his boss, Russell Roark, that I was going to speak with Collins soon. That fact would be important shortly.

We started discussing the charges against Charles. Sgt. Collins told Charles that he still wanted Charles to sign a statement against his wife, Tshona. Charles continued to refuse. Charles told Collins that Tshona did not tell him that she was involved in the death of Dr. Sunshine, nor that she had any knowledge of the crime. Charles told Collins that nothing had changed from their first meeting, and that Charles had nothing to offer.

Sgt. Collins then told Charles, "Your wife's family is nothing but a bunch of crack heads. You are better than this." The trick of alienating the witnesses was picked up by Charles immediately.

Sgt. Collins then started telling Charles that he "could give the statement now and get it over with." That did not work with Charles; Charles got defensive and loud.

Charles started talking about Suhail, the call he made from Atlanta telling Collins to come inspect the car, the attorney who Collins had sent to Charles, and other acts of indiscretion that the authorities had committed.

Now I thought I better get involved. I wanted to plant a seed, and then go for the jugular.

I said to Sgt. Collins, "This charge against Charles is a misdemeanor. If Tshona takes a plea, or is found guilty as a result of a trial, are you going to drop the charges against Charles?" Collins said yes. That proved that the charge against Charles had no merit; they charged Charles in order to try to get him to sign a statement against his wife, tried to scare and/ or intimidate Charles, and get their hands on the 1994 Lexus. They really had no intention of going to trial. The charges were baseless, and Collins knew it.

There was no probable cause to arrest Charles. Tshona never gave a statement. Tshona never implicated Charles by telling anyone that she confided to Charles any information she knew about the death of Dr. Sunshine. Charles never said she told him anything. The warrant to arrest Charles was worthless, and we were hoping to have the opportunity to prove that.

As Sgt. Collins admitted that the charges against Charles would be dropped if Tshona went to jail, I had the big question ready.

I said to Sgt. Collins, "Did you know there was another black Lexus out the night Dr. Sunshine was killed?"

Collins leaned back in his chair and said, "Do you have the VIN (vehicle identification number)?"

I had written the vehicle identification number from the 1993 on a piece of paper. I was just waiting for the right time. I handed the paper with the identification number written on the paper to Collins and said, "Yes I do."

Sgt. Collins was shocked. He thought he was being flippant when he asked for the identification number, and that would shut me up. I guess he thought I was going to just pacify Charles and not be able to expose the corruption we were seeing. Maybe he thought that anyone who found out a little about the people involved would back away from the fray. Well, I was not from the area and was not going to get caught up in the incestuous political maneuvering of this pompous lackey.

Sgt. Collins looked at the piece of paper. He became quiet. He then turned to his right and took a manila folder off the credenza behind his desk. Sgt. Collins turned back around, remaining in his chair. He placed the manila folder on the desk in front of Charles and me. Collins opened the manila folder and inside the folder were at least five or six Polaroid photographs of a wrecked 1993 Lexus. The photographs appeared to have been taken on a car lot, and the black Lexus had been backed against a fence. The photos were of inferior quality, but the damage to the car was quite evident. The headlight and fog light on the passenger side were crushed. The fender on the passenger side was damaged beyond repair, and the hood was also damaged. Both the hood and the fender would have to be replaced.

I asked Sgt. Collins if he had investigated the 1993 black Lexus. That vehicle matched the description of the vehicle observed by the witness. Sgt. Collins stated that the wrecked vehicle, which matched the description of the vehicle identified by the witness, did not match the profile of a vehicle that had hit a pedestrian or a man on a bicycle. That was not true. I had investigated hundreds of vehicle and pedestrian accidents. My reports had been admitted as evidence in many court proceedings, even overturning the findings of an officer of the SC Highway Patrol. The damage to the 1993 was consistent with a vehicle hitting a pedestrian, or a man on a bicycle. So, Collins, who was the lead investigator, made sure the vehicle was not inspected, fingerprinted, documented, or towed away. The vehicle was supposed to disappear. It almost did.

Charles and I looked more closely at the pictures, then at each other. We knew that Sgt. Collins had no advance warning when we were coming to see him, and that there was no reason for Collins to have removed that folder from the Sunshine files which was on the floor next to his right foot. He removed the folder from the file, and the photographs in the manila folder did not make it back into the file. Years later, as a result of a Freedom of Information Act request, I inspected the entire file and the photos of the 1993 Lexus were not in the file. I was told by Sheridan Spoon, the attorney for the SC Department of Public Safety, that Collins had the file and he was to deliver the file for my inspection. I assumed that Collins removed the photographs of the 1993 Lexus, the one he photographed at Hi-Line Imports, the same vehicle which was not on record as having been in the inventory at Hi- Line Imports when Collins and the other police agencies approached

Suhail. So, who was working for whom?

When Charles saw the photographs he said, "That is the car I saw last December at Hi-Line." Collins knew we were on to him.

Charles then told Sgt. Collins that he (Charles) did not authorize Sgt. Collins to take the 1994 Lexus to South Carolina. Charles told Sgt. Collins that the signature on the authorization was a forgery. I had not inspected the document, but since Sgt. Collins had been caught up in one part of the cover-up, everything else was on the table. Sgt. Collins denied forging the name. Charles told Collins that he (Charles) told Sgt.

Collins to come to Atlanta and look at the car. Charles knew the car did not hit anyone, and Charles was offering it to Sgt. Collins to inspect, not to commandeer.

Sgt. Collins knew that his cover had been blown. Charles and I knew that would be the last time we would talk to Collins. I convinced Charles to leave, but that would be only the beginning of revelations about Sgt. Collins.

I went back to my office and called Sandra Lambright. Sandra was Tshona's aunt, her mother's (Forcina's) sister. She operated a beauty salon called NY Innovations. On the evening before the accident, Tshona was with Sandra and her daughter Mamchu at Appleby's Restaurant in the northeast area of Columbia. Tshona came home after leaving the restaurant. Charles had told me earlier that Mamchu then began calling Tshona and tried to get Tshona to come out with her to go to a party at the Sheraton Hotel in Columbia. The party for Jermaine O'Neal was a basketball fan's dream. Local player makes good. All the blacks in town who followed basketball would be there. They wanted to be seen in the place with Jermaine.

Sandra told me that she had not spoken to Charles since his arrest, which was about six months prior to my call. Since her niece Tshona was married to Charles, it seemed out of the ordinary. I told Sandra that I had been retained by Charles, and I had information that would help Tshona. Sandra told me that her family had retained Chip Price, an attorney in Greenville, South Carolina, to represent Tshona. Sandra would give Mr. Price my telephone number.

Charles was being represented by Todd Rutherford, and Charles had not been given a preliminary hearing after having been arrested six months earlier. Charles told me that he had been in touch with the secretary for Todd Rutherford; her name was Melissa. Melissa told Charles that Chip Price had sent a letter to Rutherford wanting to see the paperwork on the case, but Rutherford had sent nothing to Mr. Price. That was because Rutherford had only filed a motion for discovery, and had done nothing else. It was later learned that the paperwork in Rutherford's file consisted of only the motion for discovery and newspaper clippings. I was with Charles when he picked up the file and I saw that the file was empty. This was a very high-profile death case. Charles had been arrested six months previously, and the prosecution had not given Rutherford any documents even though five months earlier Rutherford had requested the documents. Charles said Rutherford just did not care, and did not think his client had the intelligence to help himself stay out of jail.

I called Melissa myself. She told me that Rutherford had been in contact with the prosecutor, Johnny Gasser, every day. Melissa stated there was no discovery evidence in the file (even after five months) and that the prosecutor would be sending information on the case ten days before Charles' trial was to begin. She stated that Rutherford told her that was the best way to handle the case.

Rutherford really said that? The case was a high-profile death case, and the defense attorney was only going to spend ten days on preparation?

Melissa further stated that nothing would be done until the trial court date was set. Rutherford did not want anyone

36

to "push the envelope. Todd knows how to handle the case and does not want Charles to hire a private investigator to work on the case." Push the envelope? They did not want the truth to come out. They wanted some kind of deal, a quick plea, a false implication, and a conviction that would garner votes for the prosecutor and money for political races from the Jewish community. Rutherford was a member of the SC House of Representatives, and catered to persons with the means to keep him in the statehouse. And guess who was supposed to deliver it to them? Charles Outlaw. The authorities were going to be the hero for prosecuting Charles, but they persecuted him instead. Charles refused to play their game, and they were very upset with him.

Why was Rutherford not obtaining the discovery material from the prosecution? Why had Charles not had a preliminary hearing for six months? Why did Rutherford ignore Chip Price, who was representing the co-defendant? Why did Rutherford not want a private investigator to help Charles since Rutherford was doing nothing except telling his secretary he was talking with the prosecutor?

From this point on, I was living and breathing the case. In criminal cases, the first thing I did was to find mistakes made by the arresting agency. The officers have supervisors breathing down their necks, and they want someone convicted of a crime. All the truth they needed was enough to convince a jury that the person might have committed the crime. The authorities had convinced themselves that a jury might buy what they were selling. The more work I did with Charles, the more I realized that if the case went to trial, and if Charles had a good attorney, no jury would buy their story. The prosecution needed a plea without telling the defense everything they knew.

That happens all the time. Discovery motions are challenged when the defense attorney believes that more information is available than the prosecution is revealing. I would not know until later what the prosecution would give up, and I was anxious to see if their information and my information were the same.

Late in the afternoon of May 5, 2001, Charles called me at the office. He was talking about the pictures we saw that Collins had behind his desk, the photos of the 1993 Lexus. Charles wanted to know if Sgt. Collins asked for the repair report from Suhail when he saw the 1993 Lexus, wrecked, on the car lot on October 20, 2000. Evidently Collins had to see the wrecked 1993 Lexus before Suhail went through his records to determine that he had sold the 1994 Lexus to Charles. The record of the acquisition of the 1993 Lexus was also in Suhail's records. Suhail's records would show that he acquired the 1993 and the 1994 from the same auto auction near the same time. If Collins looked at the records, he would have seen the record of both cars coming into South Carolina. The reports from Collins falsely asserted that Charles' car, the 1994 Lexus, was the only black Lexus acquired by Suhail or sold by Suhail before the date of the accident. Charles' car was, in fact, the only one sold just before the accident, and it still had paper tags. The fact was that the 1993 Lexus was not sold, but was being used by the dealership to be driven around, just as Charles' car was when it was found parked in Orangeburg in August 2000.

The next day I picked up the photos of Charles' car that I took at the impound area. I took the photos over to Jimmy Winders at Leon Jones Insurance Company so Mr. Winders could compare these photos to his recollection of the condition of the 1994 Lexus when Charles initially brought it to him. Mr. Winders told me that the red mark on the bumper was not on the bumper when he first saw the car. Neither were the gouges and the majority of the scratches. The fog lamp was not missing. Mr. Winders also stated that based upon the photos I showed him of Charles' car, he did not think that Charles' car hit a person riding a bicycle.

I got back to my office and called Charles to tell him about the meeting with Mr. Winders. Charles was upset that the four local television stations had branded him as the criminal. Charles also talked about friends and others telling him that he was the one who was in the car that killed Dr. Sunshine. Charles felt like his life was ruined.

We discussed the showing of the wrecked vehicle on the television news. People that had seen the 1994 Lexus after the date of the accident, told Charles that his car did not hit anybody, and that the car on television was not the same car as Charles' car. We wondered how the media outlets could show a wrecked black Lexus on television and identify the car as the one that belonged to Charles. That was a no-brainer. The media outlets had access to pictures of a wrecked black Lexus to show on the news. It could not have been Charles' car. It had to be the photographs of the wrecked 1993 Lexus that had been in the hands of Sgt. Tom Collins.

Later in the day I received a call from Chip Price, the attorney for Charles' wife, Tshona. Chip told me that Charles called 911 to turn in Tshona while they were in Atlanta during Thanksgiving. Chip did not trust Charles, but the only information he had received to draw that conclusion would have come from Tshona's family. Charles stopped Tshona and Forcina from leaving Atlanta during the Thanksgiving holidays. Chip did not have the opportunity, or perhaps the inclination, to talk to Charles to get the full story why Tshona refused to acknowledge anything about Dr. Sunshine's death.

Sgt. Collins began calling Laura Outlaw after Suhail told Collins that Charles had bought a black Lexus from Hi-Line Imports. Laura had called Charles and told him that the police were looking for Tshona and him in connection with the death of Dr. Sunshine. The first time Collins reached Charles by telephone, Collins said to Charles, "You were in the car that killed Dr. Sunshine." Charles did not know what Collins was talking about. Collins kept calling, wanting to see the car. Charles was out of town, and would not and did not go out of his way to go see Collins. Charles had heard about the accident, but did not keep up with the local news. He had heard that the police were looking for a white car. That was all over the news before the witness showed up by way of Ms. Sunshine. Charles had even gotten a speeding ticket since the accident, still not knowing anything about the accident. The policeman was a SC Highway Patrol officer. The officer saw Charles' car when he gave him the ticket. If the car had significant damage, or if they were looking for a black Lexus, something would have happened.

During the Thanksgiving holiday, Laura called Charles and told him that the police kept coming by her house to talk with her. Tad Reid from SLED returned and demanded information from Laura about herself (that was the incident when Reid put his hand on his weapon to intimidate Laura). Laura was not being investigated nor being arrested. She had nothing to offer. She knew that Charles was not involved in the death of Dr. Sunshine, and that his car had struck no one. Laura saw that car all the time after Charles had bought the car. Laura told the police that Charles was in Atlanta for Thanksgiving so they would leave her alone.

Collins informed Laura that Charles would not make it safely back to South Carolina. Collins told Laura ". the police will ambush Charles" when Charles returned to South Carolina.

After Charles was contacted by phone repeatedly by Collins, he started asking Tshona what went on that night Dr. Sunshine was killed. Charles knew his car was not involved, but he did not know if she knew anything.

Tshona would not budge. Charles got frustrated. Tshona and Forcina acted like they wanted to leave in the car. So, Charles called 911 and told the operator that his wife was wanted as a suspect in the death of Dr. Sunshine, and that the police in Columbia, South Carolina wanted to look at his car. Charles gave the address where he was, the police arrived, Charles was arrested, Tshona was arrested, and Charles' car was taken away.

So, Chip Price's lack of confidence in Charles was based on the fact that Charles called the police, and in effect, turned Tshona in to the police. Charles certainly did not expect to be arrested. He did not know there was a warrant for his arrest. Why would he think so?

The police in South Carolina had a field day with the fact that Charles was in Atlanta. They told the press that Charles and Tshona were escaping, running from the authorities, and painted them as the black equivalent of Bonnie and Clyde.

I told Chip that Charles had retained me, and that I would be glad to help on Tshona's behalf. I told him that Charles' attorney, Todd Rutherford, was not being proactive in the least. Rutherford, according to his secretary, "did not want to push the envelope" with respect to getting information from the prosecution. Rutherford used to work in the prosecutor's office, and it was evident that he was using his association with the prosecutor to his political advantage and did not want to upset that applecart. Chip told me he had a problem getting information from the prosecutor's office, and had filed a Motion for Sanctions against the Richland County Solicitor's Office because the prosecutor/solicitor, Barney Giese, was withholding exculpatory evidence.

When a defense attorney files the motion for discovery, as all defense attorneys do, the prosecutor must give the defense everything in the file, including information which would help exonerate the defendant. The prosecution wanted the defense to think it was going to be a slam dunk; they would pressure Tshona to admit to having killed Dr. Sunshine, and that would be it.

If the prosecution thought they had the car that killed Dr. Sunshine (which we knew they did not because Sgt. Collins, Charles, and I knew the truth), and they had a witness seeing Tshona Gaymon in the area at the time of the death (the postal worker witness who could not identify Tshona from a photo lineup), why did Sgt. Collins call Laura to tell her that he was sending an attorney to Charles, and why did the prosecution and the defense attorneys pressure Charles to make a statement implicating his wife?

Why did the prosecution need Charles at all? If the evidence was credible, and would stand the scrutiny of a defense attorney and an investigator, why go to all the trouble to remove evidence from the case file, the photos of the 1993 Lexus, and tamper with Charles' car? Chip told me he would be sending his file to me. He restated that the prosecutor had withheld information from him, but I told Chip their case was so full of problems that if information I had uncovered came out in an open trial, it would be national news. The prosecution did all they could to keep the truth from coming out. But it would not be enough.

Map of travel during the evening of the incident

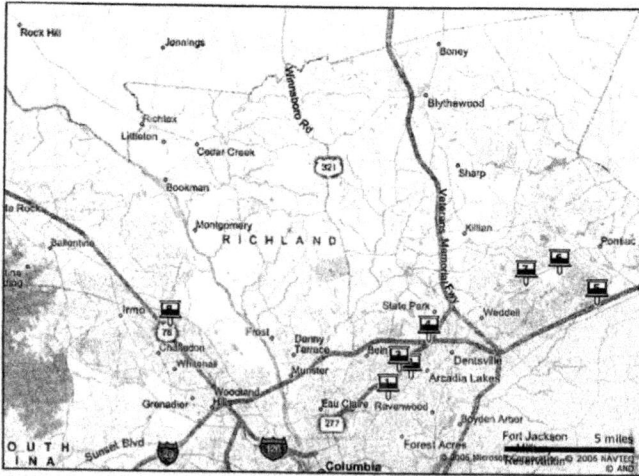

Scratch pad

1: Fantasy Island
2: Fontaine
3: I-277
4: I-20

5: Clemson Road Exit
6: Sherma's Apartment
7: Dr. Sunshine's body found
8: Charles's Apartment

Chapter Four

Larry Aaron was the next person to interview. Larry owned Aaron's Body Shop, which, coincidently, was located a block off Two Notch Road in Columbia. I had known Larry for over a year. I met him through

a former business associate of mine.

The reason I had to talk to Larry was to get his version of the conflicting information between the police and Charles. Up to that point, and for the entire time of my association with Charles, I never found Charles to lie to me. There were times when he would talk to someone, an attorney or someone on the street, and not tell me who he had been talking to, but I knew when not to ask. But he never lied; he just would not tell me who his sources were.

The big conflict with Larry had to do with Charles ever meeting Larry. Charles told me he never met Larry. The only time Charles was at Aaron's Body Shop was on the afternoon after Dr. Sunshine was killed and Charles met Ray Porter.

On the morning of the death of Dr. Sunshine, after Charles saw the scrape on his car, he was really angry at Tshona. Charles and Tshona proceeded from their apartment in the 1994 Lexus en route to Hi-Line Imports to see about Suhail fixing the damages his car had when he bought it (paint scratches and the loose lower air dam). He was also going to see if Suhail had something to take out the scrape marks on the bumper which Tshona had created. Charles was so angry at Tshona that he pulled off Main Street a few blocks from Hi-Line. He could not argue and drive at the same time. Charles got out of the car and was yelling at Tshona. A police officer then arrived. Charles did not know where the cop came from or if someone had called him. Charles showed the police officer the damage. Charles told the officer that he was on his way to the dealership, but wanted to know if he had to report the accident. The officer told Charles that the damage to the car was not enough to have to report the accident. He said, ". . . that is minor. Don't worry about it" and the police officer gave Charles a form to file with his insurance company.

Charles left that paper in the car. He thought the officer had given him something to prove that Charles did talk to the police and report the damage to his car to the authorities. Charles told me the officer's name was on the paper. Charles did not know at the time that a man across the street working at the temporary employment service, a man named James Brown, was there and saw Charles with the police officer. Mr. Brown was a black male and appeared to be in his mid-forties.

He was employed at the Veterans Administration Hospital in Columbia, but was working at that temporary service agency on a part-time basis. After the policeman left, Charles drove the 1994 Lexus across the street where Mr. Brown was working. Tshona had gone across the street to use the telephone at James Brown's office. Charles was still mad at Tshona because he did not believe she scraped a barrier, even though that was what it looked like. Charles wanted more information. Charles left the car and walked to Hi-Line Imports, which was about a block away. When Charles got to Hi-Line Imports, Suhail gave Charles an extra key and told Charles to bring the car over and let him look at it. Suhail told Charles that he would fix the previous damage, scratches, and the hanging air dam; he also said he could buff out the scrape on the bumper that Tshona was responsible for.

Charles walked back to the temporary labor office and found Tshona there with Sandra Lambright, (Tshona's aunt, Forcina's sister), who arrived to take Tshona with her. Charles found out that Tshona had called Sandra from James Brown's office. Tshona told Sandra that she would be all right, and that Sandra could go home, so Sandra left.

Mr. Brown looked at Charles' car. Charles pointed out the scrape on the bumper, the horizontal scrape, not vertical as in a pedestrian accident. Tshona told Mr. Brown that she scraped a wall at the Sheraton, and also an SUV which had a big chrome front bumper. Mr. Brown said he did not see any damage that looked like a collision with a person or a bicycle, and neither did the police officer.

About three months after Charles was released from jail in December 2000, Charles received a telephone call from James Brown. Mr. Brown asked if Charles was the same guy that he saw that day in late September, arguing with his wife. James Brown had recognized Charles and Tshona from the photo on television. Mr. Brown told Charles that the police had been harassing him, and that the authorities had been coming to his house and job. He said that he told the police he saw the 1994 Lexus which Charles was driving, and the car did not look like it hit anyone. Mr. Brown also stated that the police told him that they had been watching Charles and Tshona that morning, which was why the police were in the area.

Years later I interviewed James Brown at his home, and he told me the same thing that Charles had said; Mr. Brown had been told that the police had been watching Charles and Tshona on that morning when Mr. Brown saw them arguing across the street from his work. Mr. Brown also told me that the authorities wrote a statement for Brown to sign and the authorities left out parts of the information that would exonerate Charles.

When Charles and I looked inside the car at the impound facility, the paper the policeman gave him was gone. James Brown saw the police officer at Charles' car and could testify that Charles "did report this to a police officer," and that the form given to Charles by the policeman did exist.

After Sandra Lambright left, Charles and Tshona left the temporary

employment office and James Brown, and drove to Hi-Line Imports. Suhail looked at the car and told Charles that the scrape on the bumper could be buffed and painted, but Suhail did not do that kind of repairs at his business. Suhail referred Charles to Larry Aaron, at Aaron's Body Shop.

Charles left Suhail en route to Aaron's Body Shop. Larry was not there, but Larry's assistant, Ray Porter, was there. Ray did body work, and Ray stated that he was not authorized to give any estimates. Ray did not have the experience to do that. Ray looked at the car, and Charles gave his telephone number to Ray. Ray said he would have Larry call Charles. That was midday Saturday, close to six hours after Dr. Sunshine was found on the side of the road. Since Charles could not see Larry, who was authorized to give him an estimate on the damage, Charles went home.

The following Monday, Charles received a telephone call from Larry Aaron. Larry told me that he remembered seeing a note with Charles' name and telephone number, and that Larry called that number and talked to Charles. Larry told Charles to take the car over to Leon Jones Insurance Company located on Beltline Boulevard in Columbia. Larry told Charles that he knew Jimmy Winders very well, and said that regardless of the deductible, the car would get fixed and Charles probably would not have to pay the deductible.

Charles and Tshona then went to see Mr. Winders. Tshona told Mr. Winders same story about the damage to the car, and she never changed her story. Suhail had told

Charles that the scratches on the car as well as the air dam hanging down would be fixed at Larry Aaron's, so Charles made sure that Mr. Winders knew to put that on the report for Larry Aaron to see.

Even though I had not gotten the file from Chip Price, I knew Larry well enough to go talk to him. Larry literally lived at the body shop. He had a separate door that led to his personal living quarters. Larry was what you would call a good old boy. He appeared scruffy and acted like he was not paying attention to you, but Larry was smart. Larry would seem inattentive to you, telling you what was wrong with your car, and it seemed as if he was talking past you. He knew the body shop business and the insurance business. He repaired a vehicle of mine which was damaged by a municipal truck, so I had dealings with Larry and Ray.

I had seen Larry talk to people. I stopped by there many times to check on my car, and sometimes to chat if I were driving by. Larry was direct and sometimes short with people, as though he did not care if he got their business or not. He would cut you off on the telephone and hang up before you thought the conversation was over. Larry had a big pick-up truck, big boat, and he had a fast street car out back. It did not seem that Larry was lacking for money, and people with money did not impress him. He lived his life the way he wanted to, yelled at the help from time to time, and if he had been out late, or all night, Larry would be asleep in his quarters until past noon. He would tell me what he had done the night before and I had to laugh. He made no secret that he had been out partying. He was almost like a cartoon character, and he was crazy like a fox.

Larry told me that on the Monday following the accident he was approached by a black man driving a black Lexus. The girlfriend of the Lexus driver was following him in another car. The black man was described as having dreadlocks which almost touched his shoulders. Larry said that the black man told him that the Lexus had a busted headlight. He also stated that the driver of the Lexus did not have any gold teeth in the front of his mouth.

Charles Outlaw did not have dreadlocks. According to Charles, having dreadlocks was a style used by Jamaicans and Haitians but blacks weaved their hair in cornrows. Also, Charles had prominent gold teeth in the front of his mouth. That was one of the first things I noticed, and that was the reason people put gold teeth in the front of their mouth, to be noticed.

Larry told me that he saw the couple for a few minutes and they left.

He did not give them an estimate.

Larry told me he did not take much time looking at the car. According to Larry, the car had a broken fog lamp and busted out headlight. He told me he walked around the car and saw the dented hood and bent fender. Charles' car never had that damage.

I asked Larry if he remembered calling someone that morning. Larry told me that he remembered seeing a note that Ray had left, and calling someone, and that he referred the person to their insurance company, Leon Jones Insurance. That was Charles who Larry had called.

I asked Larry about the initial report to the media that Dr. Sunshine had been struck by a white Lexus. The police came to him to see if he had repaired any white Lexus vehicles. Larry had told them no. For almost a month the media reported that the police were looking for a white vehicle. Bulletins were printed looking for a white Lexus. Supposedly there were white smudges on the bicycle and the police reported it. Larry told me that when the police told him that white smudges were on the bicycle, Larry told the police that if a Lexus had struck a vehicle, there were so many layers of clear coat on top of the original color of the car that the impact would transfer as white. The real color of the car would not be known. Larry told me that he told the police, "Y'all are real dumb asses" for not knowing about the color transfer of the paint.

It was later learned from the report from SLED that the evidence at the scene linking a Lexus to the crime was a broken Lexus vanity license plate, which was at the scene of the hit and run. The license plate would be placed on the front bumper of a vehicle. Charles' car never had a vanity license plate. Suhail confirmed that when we met him. Plus, the police were running around looking at and photographing white Lexus vehicles. I wondered if the people in power planted white Lexus as a red herring so the real criminals would never be caught. I was not alone in that thought. The postal worker messed up their plans.

According to the authorities, the other piece of evidence linking Charles' car to the crime scene was broken glass from a fog light cover. (It will be shown later that the glass fragments were sent to the FBI laboratory, and the results came back stating that there was no definitive evidence to identify that piece of glass as being glass that came from a Lexus fog lamp cover, or automotive glass.) When SLED made their findings from their lab, they contradicted the FBI findings. I guess authorities in South Carolina think their forensics laboratories are more advanced and accurate than those at the FBI facility. (See Appendix)

When Charles got the FBI report from me that I received from Chip Price, I showed Charles the contradiction. He was livid. It was at that time Charles began making phone calls to persons without telling me. I told him that his defense needed to be conducted in a methodical manner, and I would not be doing anything of any significance without telling him. But sometimes Charles got so wrapped up he would call people and vent.

Don't Get Arrested in South Carolina

On a Sunday afternoon, soon after I got the discovery information from Chip Price, I was in the office working on the case when Charles called. He told me that he had called the FBI office in Columbia to vent about how the local authorities had treated him and to see if he could get any attention from them. Charles wanted me to call and talk to the same agent he had been contacting, so I told Charles I would.

I called the agent at the number Charles gave me. The agent was very nice, and I apologized for calling him on a Sunday. I explained that my client asked that I make the call, so it was a hoop jump for me. The agent was the one who received the material from the authorities in South Carolina to send to the FBI lab. The shards of glass were sent, along with parts of Harry Sunshine's bicycle. The agent told me that the authorities in South Carolina alleged that the markings on the bicycle were from white paint transferred from the vehicle which struck Dr. Sunshine. Well, Larry Aaron told the authorities that they could not determine the color of the vehicle because the transfer of clear coat would always be white. The FBI agent told me that he was not impressed with the laboratory at the South Carolina Law Enforcement Division, and he made other disparaging comments about their lab and their "findings." The agent told me that the scraping on the bicycle parts were not the result of any vehicle striking the vehicle; the markings were a result of road debris.

And of course, the fog lamp cover for the 1993 vehicle was interchangeable with the fog lamp cover of the 1994 Lexus owned by Charles. When Charles and I examined and photographed the 1994 Lexus, the fog lamp assembly was missing. The wires had been cut. The authorities only needed the cover to match any shards of glass. Now the authorities had access to both Charles' fog lamp cover, and the fog lamp cover from the 1993 Lexus. They were the same; they matched, and interchanged at will. There would be no need to question the chain of custody of the missing 1994 fog lamp. It would be a waste of time, but I assumed we would address the issue at some point in time.

Of course, the authorities "investigating" the death of Dr. Sunshine would never publish these findings to the general public. The newspapers and electronic media did not know that their "evidence" was not evidence at all. The media outlets were being duped. The authorities certainly did not want a trial, not for Tshona or for Charles.

There was a method to their madness. We knew why they were doing it. We just wanted a trial.

I knew that the SC Highway Department kept records of insurance coverage for automobile dealers. I figured that since the 1993 Lexus had been wrecked, which Charles confirmed in December 2000, and Sgt. Collins had seen in October 2000, the repairs to the damage would be paid from an insurance policy carried by Hi-Line Imports.

My research revealed that the insurance company used by Hi-Line Imports was Evergreen National Indemnity Company. The company had the coverage on the vehicle from September 13, 1999 through September 13, 2000. It was a "garage policy" which covered all cars on the lot. The local agent would have had the list of the cars on the lot at any given time. Evergreen had some information about the principals of the company but we did not need to know their identities.

A call to the claims department revealed that Hi-Line Imports had filed a couple of claims during that year, but not one for the 1993 Lexus. Since the accident occurred after the policy had expired, it would not help.

I then called the SC Highway Department to get information about Hi-Line Imports. A lady told me that Hi-Line Imports had two locations, one on Main Street and one on Two Notch Road. The location on Two Notch Road had their dealer license canceled on January 31, 2001, which was five months before my call. The location on Main Street was still active. She told me that Companion Insurance was the company that covered the vehicles at Hi-Line Imports, and she gave me the policy number. She also gave me the name of the local agent, which was Allied Assurance Company. I called Allied Assurance Company and talked with a lady named Clara. I learned that Allied Assurance Company did have the coverage for Hi-Line Imports. She said the coverage was blanket coverage, and that no claims had been presented since September 2000. I specifically asked about the 1993 Lexus, and gave Clara the vehicle identification number. She told me that there was no record of any claim for repairs on the 1993 Lexus from Hi-Line Imports.

So, not only did Suhail get the 1993 Lexus repaired privately, but the cost of the repair was paid without making a claim to the insurance company. The advantage to Suhail repairing the 1993 Lexus privately would be to keep his insurance premiums from increasing and keeping the extent and nature of the damage from being revealed. But maybe Suhail did not have the 1993 Lexus repaired; what if the vehicle was repaired privately by the person responsible for causing the death of Dr. Sunshine? Either way, the car was on the lot of Hi-Line Imports in August 2000, loaned out, and damaged; the damage was observed by Charles, Suhail, and Sgt. Collins; the vehicle was repaired, evidence of the damage was listed on the computer at Hi-Line Imports as having been repaired, and was now being driven by Anthony Kelly.

Do you think the authorities wanted the public to know that the car was repaired privately? The existence of the vehicle had been kept from the public.

The photographs of the 1993 Lexus were taken on October 20, 2000. That information was revealed to me by Sgt. Collins. Suhail did not give a statement to the authorities until December 1, 2000, a few days after the arrest of Charles Outlaw. Suhail's statement did not mention the fact that the 1993 Lexus was observed by the authorities on October

20. The only black Lexus Suhail mentioned on his statement was the one purchased by Charles Outlaw a few days before the accident. The reports from all three agencies were inconsistent; one noted the 1993 Lexus, the others did not.

Why did the authorities wait over a month to get a statement from Suhail? They took statements from others on the spot, at the same time as the initial interview. That made no sense at all, but was not surprising. Statements should be taken as soon as possible because the witness would forget things. But if Suhail was being told what to put on a statement, it would not matter what he remembered. What mattered was that he signed a statement placed in front of him regardless of what he remembered.

If Suhail did not sign a statement until after Charles was arrested, were the authorities going to do what they thought they could get away with and fill in the blanks later?

Chapter Five

Ray Porter worked for Larry Aaron. Ray had worked doing body work before. He was a short pudgy guy. I sold Ray a car of mine before the accident, so I had the opportunity to know Ray personally. I would come by the shop or he would come by my office and he made the payments on the car. His wife was a very pretty young lady, and he had an infant in the house. His wife's father held some administrative post in a small town outside Columbia, and helped his daughter in a tanning salon in town. The father seemed to be very politically correct and kept a tight rein on his daughter, even though she was married and had a child.

Ray often complained to me that Larry slept all day. I knew that part of Larry's life; he partied a lot, but Larry was very good at body work. Ray complained about Larry's managerial style, and that Larry yelled a lot at Ray if Larry was in a bad mood.

I called Ray to ask him about the visit that Charles and Tshona made to the shop on Saturday, less than six hours after Dr. Sunshine was found dead. Ray told me that between 10 a.m. and 11a.m. on September 2000, a black male drove to the shop in a black Lexus and that he did not remember seeing any dreadlocks or gold teeth. Ray told the man that he was not authorized to give any estimate on the car; Larry would have to do that. The man gave Ray a telephone number to give to Larry for Larry to call.

That was exactly what Charles told me. I called Charles, and I told Charles about my conversation with Ray; Charles said, "That was me. I talked to Ray Porter and gave him my number to call." Charles said again that Ray did not give him an estimate on the damage to his car, and that Charles would have to talk to Larry.

Ray knew me. Ray knew the type work I did, and if he lied, he knew I would find out. But now we had two different cars going to the body shop. Charles only went once. Tshona did not follow Charles in a different car; she was in the car with him. They both had just left Sandra Lambright, and Sandra saw them both drive off from James Brown en route to Hi-Line Imports.

The material I received from Chip Price contained two different statements from Ray Porter given to the authorities. Ray told the authorities in one statement that Charles was the man who came back on the following Monday. Larry's description of the man he saw, a man having no gold teeth, did not match Ray's description. That was because Charles never went to see Larry Aaron; Larry directed Charles to Jimmy Winders by telephone, not in person.

Jimmy Winders gave us copies of the insurance photos, but refused to give us a copy of the report. Mr. Winders said Charles was not entitled to the report. Charles' car clearly had a full headlight and the glass from the fog light was also in the photograph. The photo did not clearly show the entire fog light, but Charles did tell me that the lamp was cracked diagonally as a result of the scrape, and Charles taped the glass to keep it from falling out. According to Charles, no glass was missing. Also, the bracket holding the fog lamp was clearly visible in the photograph, but the authorities said a broken piece of a bracket was at the scene. If there was a piece of bracket at the scene of the accident, it would not have been from Charles' car.

I wanted a trial in the worst way. I had no way of knowing how much worse it would get.

First Citizens Bank had financed the 1994 Lexus for Charles. I went to the local branch located across Main Street from Hi-Line Imports. I identified myself and told them I needed a copy of the finance sheet for Charles' car, the 1994 Lexus. The bill of sale which showed the sale price of the car did not match the financing sheet that Charles had. The bank showed a sales price of $16,995. The finance sheet showed the price as $18,495. Charles did not know about the discrepancy.

On May 9, 2001 I called Suhail to interview him. There were many issues to address with him. Suhail refused to talk to me. He said that I was not just a friend of Charles and that I was a private investigator. I guess word got out. It's a small world after all.

On May 11, 2001 I received the discovery material from Chip Price. There was quite a bit of material in the package, but Chip told me he asked for sanctions against the prosecutor Gasser because Chip did not get the entire file. Since Todd Rutherford had produced nothing for Charles, I would use the information from Tshona's attorney to help both of them.

I learned that a preliminary hearing was scheduled for Charles for May 14, 2001. I showed up at the hearing site at the magistrate court. Sgt. Collins was there with the family of Dr. Sunshine. It was then I found out that this preliminary hearing, the one that Charles had been wanting for six months, had been postponed. I was going to find out what was going on, and the result was not surprising.

Now I had time to digest the discovery material I received from Chip, which was quite interesting. A report from SLED stated that glass taken from the crime scene matched the glass in Charles' fog lamp. Of course, they would say that. They had access to two structurally identical cars having interchangeable parts. One was damaged as a result of a pedestrian accident, and one was not. Their mantra must have been, "Use whatever you need to use to make the good car have damage like the other car." The problem the authorities had was they tried to cover up so much that they left out things as a result of their arrogance. They never intended for the case to go to trial. They threw false allegations out and the media gobbled it up like pigs in slop.

Back to the fog light. When Charles and I inspected the 1994 Lexus in the impound facility, the fog lamp was missing as was a panel behind the fog light. The discovery material had no evidence of photographs of the condition of Charles' car upon recovery of the vehicle by authorities in Georgia. The authorities in Georgia turned the car over to the authorities in South Carolina. The authorities knew where the wrecked 1993 Lexus was parked, and they had the 1994 Lexus at the impound facility.

The discovery material had no evidence of a chain of custody for Charles' car. Charles would be held hostage by the prosecutor's office because Charles would not play ball with them. They fed their story to the media. They made Charles suffer. They restricted his travel. They made him report to a bail agent. They made him go to roll call. Sgt. Collins stated to a judge that the matter would not go to trial as the judge was signing the warrant for Charles' arrest. A tag number was given for Charles' car on the arrest warrant. Charles' car had paper tags. Collins had never seen the car. Sgt. Collins took conflicting information from Larry Aaron and Ray Porter, and had Ray Porter give two statements to meet whatever criteria he wanted to convince the judge that he, Collins, was telling the truth. Then the judge signed the warrant for the arrest of Charles, dismissing the fact that Collins had not seen the car. (See Appendix)

When Charles was arrested, he was transported back to Columbia by Sgt. Collins. Charles told Collins that he knew nothing and did not know why he was being arrested. Charles reminded Collins that Collins accused Charles of being in the car that killed Dr. Sunshine. He also reminded him that the reason he did not drive back to South Carolina was because the paper tag from Hi-Line Imports had expired and Charles did not want to drive it, so he told them to ask Sgt. Collins to come to Atlanta and look at the car.

Sgt. Collins continued to harp on the fact that the authorities did not want Charles; they wanted Tshona. He said the charges against Charles were going to be dropped after they got a conviction on Tshona, and that Charles had nothing to worry about. Collins had found out that Charles was originally from New York. Charles told Collins that he was going to have to hire an attorney. Collins told Charles that Charles did not need to hire any out of state or New York attorney; Sgt. Collins told Charles that he would get an attorney for him. Charles knew the offer was unethical and unusual. Corruption was a way of life in New York and Charles figured that since he had no political or criminal connections in Columbia or South Carolina, he was fair game.

Charles was placed in the Alvin S. Glenn Detention Center in Columbia. He was charged with Failing to Report a Traffic Accident having Property Damage in Excess of One Thousand Dollars. The charge was not a felony. The charge was an administrative charge, and no amount of fine was listed in the statute. It was administrative, like not renewing your license. The bond amount was $250,000.00. Excessive, yes. Obscenely excessive. They were trying to scare Charles to do what they wanted, lie on a statement that his wife told him she killed Dr. Sunshine. She never told him she did that, and he never signed the statement.

On the following day, Laura Outlaw received a telephone call from Sgt. Collins. Sgt Collins told Ms. Outlaw that "he" was going to help Charles. Laura said, "What are you going to do to help Charles? You are the one who put him in jail for something he did not do." Collins told Laura that he was going to have the bond reduced, as if Collins had any power to do that. The judge sets the bond. The prosecutor makes the case for the bond. Collins also told her that he, Sgt. Collins, was sending Charles an attorney.

Charles had no idea that Collins was telling that to his mother, and furthermore did not know that Collins was sending him an attorney.

Laura then got a call from Jerry Finney, an attorney in Columbia. Mr. Finney told Laura Outlaw that he knew Charles was in trouble, and that he (Finney) was going to the jail to see Charles. Laura initially thought Charles had called Finney, but Charles did not know Finney. Laura did not realize at the time that Sgt. Collins had sent Finney to go see Charles, evidently to try to get that elusive statement implicating Tshona.

Laura then got a call from Sgt. Collins. Collins told Laura that he had sent Finney to see Charles. Collins admitted it. This law enforcement officer arranged for a private attorney to be hired by a person he had arrested. Collins did not hide the fact that he did this. Collins implied to Laura that he was going to take care of Charles. But the authorities still wanted Charles to sign a statement against Tshona.

Collins continued, and asked Laura to tell Charles ". . . to cooperate with Finney. I had the bond lowered." Laura asked Collins how he got the bond reduced. Collins stated he was trying to "help" and that she would be receiving a call later in the day.

Jerry Finney showed up to talk to Charles at the jail. Charles did not know that Finney was coming to see him. The conversation was not very long, and Charles made arrangements to see Finney after Charles got out of jail.

Later in the day Laura got a call from the jail. The caller stated that ". . . your son will be going in front of a judge for a bond reduction, but this was not on the calendar."

Laura went to the jail. She was told that Judge Womble was to be the judge, which was said by the jail personnel to be out of the ordinary. Womble's wife and sister were in the courtroom. Upon arriving in the courtroom Laura was asked by one of the jail employees if she and her family were "celebrities" because they had never seen Judge Womble at the jail, and that Womble's presence was out of the ordinary.

Laura then received a call from her cousin, Happy. Happy told her that she needed to get Charles out of that jail for his own safety. That relative named the original suspect, John Brown, as the person who was involved in the death of Dr. Sunshine. Judge Davis, who signed the original warrant, stated to me that during his first conversations with Collins, John Brown and his brother, K.C., were the original suspects named by Sgt. Collins. Laura told me that her cousin, known as "Happy," described John Brown as a "dirty nigger." Happy was a black man, and knew John Brown and his family very well.

Neither Laura nor Happy, who owned Happy Daddy Towing Service, knew that Collins had named the same person as the original suspect to Judge Davis. Laura's cousin was well known in the black community, and knew a number of persons in law enforcement. He got arrested for possession of stolen goods, but told Laura that he had been brought most of that stuff by law enforcement officers in the area. So, her cousin knew the crooks and the drug dealers; some wore badges, some wore ties, and some wore both.

The bond hearing commenced. Charles' bond was reduced from $250,000 to $25,000, a 90 per cent reduction. Charles still had not given a statement against Tshona, but the authorities and their minions were not through with Charles.

Charles got out of jail. Laura and her cousin, Happy, arranged for a bondsman to handle the bond. The cost of the bond would be ten percent, and Happy paid the fee to the bondsman. Jerry Finney's name was listed as the attorney for Charles, but Charles had not made any agreement or paid any money to Finney. Was Finney so anxious to have Charles as a client that he did not ask for a fee? Charles would soon find out.

Not long after Charles had gotten out of jail he went to see Jerry Finney. Laura and another relative named Frank Tolliver went with him for support.

Upon arriving at the office of Jerry Finney they all sat in a conference room. Jerry Finney said to Charles, "You seem to be in a lot of trouble. Tell me what happened."

Charles started telling the story. Charles got very animated as he repeated the story. He told Finney about the scraped fender, going to Hi-Line Imports, meeting James Brown while en route to Hi-Line Imports, getting a speeding ticket from the SC Highway Patrol when the police were looking for the killer and the officer not noticing enough damage to be suspicious, Collins accusing him of being in the car that killed Dr. Sunshine, the arrest, and the taking of his car.

Charles told Jerry Finney that Collins was trying to get him to lie and give a statement that Tshona told Charles that she was in the car. Charles told Finney that Tshona did not tell him she did anything. Finney's response was, ". . . that is not what we want to hear."

So, what did Finney want to hear? Laura and Charles both told me that they were shocked at what Finney had said.

Laura asked Finney how much he charged to represent clients, and did they have to sign a contract or something. Finney told them that he was not worried about the money, for them not to concern themselves with that. If Charles was not paying Finney, who was? Finney was not doing that for nothing. It was not a pro bono case. Laura smelled a rat. Finney tried for an hour to get Charles to say something implicating Tshona. Charles kept telling Finney he did not know anything and that Tshona did not tell him anything about the death of Dr. Sunshine. Laura told Finney that Tshona did not tell her anything either. Finney kept trying, and Charles was getting mad. Finney even gave Charles a pad and Finney told Charles to write down "…what she told you about the accident." Charles refused. He told Finney he would not lie.

The definition of suborning is "to persuade another to do wrong: to persuade somebody to commit a crime or other wrongdoing," e.g., to bribe another party to tell lies in court. The false statement Charles would be giving to Finney was to be submitted as a court document if Charles were to testify against his wife. The mere request by Finney fell under the definition.

Why did Finney want Charles to implicate Tshona? Why did Collins want Charles to implicate Tshona? What about all the cold hard evidence they told the media they had? Why did they need Charles?

Finney was getting nowhere. All Finney was doing was addressing the issue of Tshona and not the defense of Charles. Finney then told the group that he was going to go talk with his father.

His father? Jerry Finney's father was retired South Carolina Chief Justice Ernest Finney. Charles thought that since Collins was a white man, he could trust a black attorney to protect him. Charles found out that was not the case.

Finney returned and asked the group to come with him. They went into a different office. At the desk was Judge Ernest Finney. Everyone was cordial and polite, but it would not remain that way.

Jerry Finney told Judge Finney that he was unable to get Charles to furnish a statement implicating Tshona in the crime.

Judge Finney said to Charles, in front of Laura and Frank Tolliver, "Now son, you are not getting it. That is not what we want to hear."

Charles continued to tell them that Tshona, his wife, who he legally did not have to testify against, did not tell him anything about a crime.

Judge Finney banged his fist on the table as he said to Charles, "Son, you are not getting it. All you need to do is tell us she did it." Judge Finney insisted that Charles sign a statement against Tshona. When Charles told both attorneys that he ". . . was not going to lie about anything" and that Tshona had never told Charles anything about a hit and run, Judge Finney became very agitated.

Charles then asked about his car. Judge Finney stated, "You can get plenty of Lexuses; just tell us what we want to hear."

So, what did Judge Finney want to hear?

Again, Laura asked how much this would be costing them. Laura was told, "We will discuss that later. We are just trying to help your son."

Laura, Charles, and Frank then left the office. They thought it was quite unusual for an attorney to make an unsolicited visit to a jail to obtain a client, and to try to persuade Charles to falsify a statement. Charles was not asked to sign a contract or pay any fee for this attorney. Why did Collins send Finney, of all people, to see Charles?

What was the connection between Finney and Collins? Who was telling Collins to send Finney to see Charles? Collins and the other police agencies had made so many mistakes in their reports; dual statements from witnesses, refuting FBI evidence, refuting certain parts of a witness statement for their benefit, conflicting statements from the three agencies about the same event, as well as falsifying a statement from Suhail by stating that the 1994 Lexus was the only black Lexus on the lot.

All they wanted was for Charles to sign the statement and all the convoluted reports would not be exposed in court for the public to see. No one would know about the suborning of perjury.

The entire matter involved implicating Tshona and ignoring the 1993 Lexus.

Charles did not know that Sgt. Collins had told Judge Davis, before the warrant was signed, that the charges against Charles were going to be dropped before any trial could occur (which technically he could not do; only the prosecutor could do that, which added another wrinkle). Charles was never given a copy of the search warrant for his 1994 Lexus.

Charles never signed any release for the vehicle to be impounded and examined. Charles stated that someone signed his name to the release. Charles had called Sgt. Collins to have him come inspect his 1994 Lexus, dismiss him as a suspect, and leave him alone.

Judge Davis told me later that he never signed a search warrant for Charles' car. Years later I found Sgt. Collins in the office of his superior, Captain Hancock. Sgt. Collins told me that Judge Davis signed the search warrant for the car. The clerk for Judge Davis searched her books and told me that no search warrant existed.

Then there was the issue of the apartment that Charles and Tshona lived in. When Charles returned to his apartment after leaving jail, the apartment had been emptied. I contacted the apartment manager and was told that some men having dreadlocks came in and emptied the apartment while Tshona and Charles were in jail.

Laura told me they would stand by their account of the events which occurred in Finney's office.

Chapter Six

There were a number of issues that needed to be addressed.

The vehicle sold to Charles Outlaw had pre-existing scratches which, according to the authorities, were attributed to the death of Dr. Sunshine. That was not true. The scratches and the hanging air dam had been observed by the woman who rented the car a month before Charles bought the car.

The club which Tshona, Sherma, Shermica, and the cousin attended, Fantasy Island, was closed no later than 3 a.m. on the morning of the accident. That was told to me by the doorman who was working there that Friday night/Saturday morning. The black female postal worker witness saw a black female in a black Lexus from Hi-Line Imports at 5:45 a.m. A black male was the passenger. Sherma had already been taken home by that time.

Tshona stated to the police officer on Main Street on the morning after the accident that she struck a concrete barrier, which caused the scrape. The policeman saw the car and he had no suspicion that the vehicle had been in any accident other than the scrape.

Charles took the 1994 Lexus to Leon Jones Insurance to have the damage documented by Mr. Winders. At that time, Charles had no knowledge of the accident involving Dr. Sunshine, and Tshona was in the vehicle with Charles. She exhibited no signs of anxiety to Mr. Winders.

The erroneous conclusion purported by the local and state authorities that Dr. Sunshine was struck by a white vehicle was broadcast by all news outlets. The authorities were allowed, or directed, to take the false theory and feed it to the media.

The FBI report clearly stated that the slivers of glass could not positively be identified as glass from any exact source, much less from a specific type of automobile.

Suhail Najjar was in concert with the police by allowing the false story that the only black Lexus at his business was the one purchased by Charles Outlaw.

Sgt. Collins had, in his possession, photographs of the 1993 Lexus, which had been removed from the case file before the arrival of Charles and me. Collins did not offer the existence of the photos or the vehicle until I gave him the exact vehicle identification number, and then he knew he was caught.

Sgt. Collins obtained a warrant for the arrest of Charles Outlaw using false information he gave to the judge. The vehicle had a paper tag; Collins purported the vehicle had a metal tag.

Sgt. Collins obtained possession of the 1994 Lexus with no valid release from Charles Outlaw.

Sgt. Collins attempted to persuade Charles Outlaw, a criminal defendant, to hire an attorney sent to Charles by the arresting officer, Collins. Collins admitted to Laura Outlaw that he sent an attorney to Charles.

Jerry Finney approached Charles in jail as an attorney, but Finney was unsolicited and had been sent by Collins. Public Defenders are assigned. Finney was not a Public Defender.

Jerry Finney and his father, Judge Finney, attempted to have Charles implicate his wife in the death of Dr. Sunshine. Charles refused to commit perjury.

The Finneys did not ask for a contract or retainer. Subsequent attorneys for Charles have asked for retainers from $5,000.00 to $20,000.00.

In January 2001, the police chief at South Carolina State University, a pre-dominantly black school, voided the parking ticket placed on the windshield of the 1994 Lexus. The parking ticket was placed on the windshield of the vehicle in August 2000. The vehicle was parked adjacent to a dormitory at which a student was murdered within weeks of the time the 1994 Hi-Line Imports Lexus was parked at the dormitory. The South Carolina Law Enforcement Division agent working the case was advised of that information and declined to interview anyone at Hi-Line Imports.

After Charles' preliminary hearing was postponed six times, he wanted to get another attorney. Charles wanted an attorney to defend him, not to offer him up to the prosecution. Now was the time to review the discovery material Mr. Price sent to me. A selection of the material is listed below.

The statement from Suhail Najjar, dated December 1, 2000.

Suhail stated that Charles bought the 1994 Lexus on September 27, 2000 from Hi-Line Imports. Charles came to his lot three days after the purchase and Tshona was with Charles. Charles told Suhail that his wife had an accident and Charles wanted the damage to be fixed. Suhail did not mention the fact that the black 1993 Lexus existed. Suhail referred Charles to John Harris Body Shop or to Aaron's Body Shop. Suhail stated he did not remember the damage to the vehicle.

The statement appeared to have been written by someone other than Suhail.

Why did Suhail not remember the damage to the vehicle?

Why did Suhail not give a statement until December 1 when Sgt. Collins was on the premises of Hi-Line Imports on October 20, 2000 when the photographs of the 1993 Lexus were taken?

Statements by Ray Porter, November 1 & November 13,2000.

On November 1, 2000 Ray Porter stated that a customer came to the shop driving a black Lexus. There was damage to the right front fender and door post along the windshield. The damage was to the fog light in the bumper with glass missing, as well as damage to the right fender. Ray could not help the man because his boss wrote all the estimates. The police returned to Ray on November 13, 2000   to take another statement. The second statement was basically the same except that on the last line of the statement Ray was asked to estimate the damage to the car. Ray estimated the damage to the car to be between $1,000.00 and $2,000.00.

Ray was not authorized to give an estimate. The authorities came back the second time in order to get an estimate that would give them the authority to make up a charge in order to arrest Charles.

Charles told me that Ray had merely walked around the car, never bending over or getting on his knees. In order to see the fog light   he would have had to almost get onto his knees. Ray did not have   a small stomach, and he would not have been able to see the light without being on his knees. With respect to Ray saying in one of the statements by the police that glass was missing, Ray would have had to get onto his hands and knees, and be very close to the fog light cover or magnify the area to see the "slivers" of glass that were sent off to the FBI laboratory.

Ray stated that green and white marks were on the door post. Then Ray stated that it was his opinion that the "Lexus" hit something other than a vehicle. I doubt that Ray remembered green and white paint on a door post a month later, or that Ray's opinion (not being authorized to give an opinion by his boss) was to be the probable cause to arrest Charles.

Statement of Larry Aaron, November 1, 2000.

Larry Aaron stated that a black male came to get an estimate on damages on a black Lexus. The damage was to the bumper cover, right fender, and right door post. Larry was told that the accident occurred in a parking lot.

During my interview with Larry Aaron he told me that the man in the Lexus was followed by a female in another car. There was no mention of a description of the black male as having dreadlocks or having gold front teeth. Charles had prominent gold front teeth.

Warrant G638281, November 16, 2000, for Charles Outlaw.

That was for the charge of Failure to Report Certain Accident (having property damage in excess of one thousand dollars). The tag number for the Lexus was listed but Charles never had a permanent tag on the vehicle; he only had a paper tag. Suhail had the tag delivered to Hi-Line Imports from the SC Highway Department.

The Waiver of Extradition (from Georgia).

It was signed as "Charles M. Outlaw, Jr." but Charles stated he never signed the waiver. Also, Charles never signed his name in that manner. In addition to that, the extradition papers were written for a defendant named Michael Outlaw, not Charles M. Outlaw. Michael was the brother of Charles.

Statement from Sharon Keels.

Ms. Keels stated that on the morning of the accident she observed a black Lexus having a paper tag worded Hi-Line on Two Notch Road at around 5:30 a.m. on September 30, 2000. She pulled alongside the vehicle and observed a black male in the passenger seat. The driver was a black female. Sharon could not identify Tshona Gaymon from a photo lineup as the driver. The authorities tried to dismiss the part of the statement of the black male being in the car. The authorities placed Sherma Doughty in the car as the passenger. It has been acknowledged that Sherma was in the car earlier in the evening. One account had Sherma leaving the club at around 3:00 a.m. Sherma gave a statement to the authorities that she was home at 5:00 a.m. Evidently the authorities did not understand that Sherma had been out of the car for about 45 minutes before the accident, at the minimum. The authorities put Sherma back into the car. Sharon Keels saw a black man in the car.

Photos of Charles' car taken at Leon Jones Insurance.

The photographs of Charles' car taken by Jimmy Winders showed that the headlight was intact. The fog light did have a diagonal crack, acknowledged by Charles, but the photograph was not clear. The fender was scratched, but those scratches were on the car when Charles bought the car. We had two witnesses to that; the prosecution did not know about those witnesses. These witnesses, who drove the vehicle a month before the accident, submitted signed and notarized statements that the air dam was hanging and the majority of the scratches on the fender were there when they drove the car. The rest of the scratches were made by the police after the car was in their custody. Jimmy Winders was shown photographs of the vehicle which were taken at the impound facility. Winders stated that some of the paint damage, scratches, on the car were not on the car when he first saw it. Charles did not scratch his own car; the police had his car. As for damage purported to have been on the 1994 Lexus by the authorities as a result of hitting Dr. Sunshine, Jimmy Winders would have submitted that, but the evidence was not there. Now a person would understand why Jimmy Winders would not give Charles a copy of his report to the insurance company.

Statement of Jimmy Winders.

Mr. Winders stated that the only damage he remembered was to the right fender. (The photograph taken by Winders showed the fender and headlight intact). If there were other damaged areas to the car, he would have stated so.

Kimberly Black, SLED Agent, report January 25, 2001.

Kimberly Black submitted a report to Sgt. E. R. Moffat, SC Highway Patrol. The report was the result of an examination of items submitted from the bicycle ridden by Dr. Sunshine, fibers from the passenger door of Charles' vehicle, and other areas of Charles' car. The fibers were found not to be consistent with fibers from the clothing from Dr. Sunshine's clothes. The hair found under the car was animal hair. That eliminated Charles' car as having been in the accident. Also, with respect to a blue smear said to have been found on Charles' car (which was not on the car when Jimmy Winders photographed the car after the date of the accident), it was noted, "This smear has similar physical and chemical characteristics to the sneaker. The result of the examination is inconclusive." I assumed that if the case went to trial the prosecution would only read the first sentence in open court. The only sentence of any relevance was the second sentence, citing the result, not conjecture. Having Kimberly Black on the stand with a report like that would be leading a lamb to slaughter.

Kenneth H. Whitler, SLED Agent, report January 24, 2001.

The report was submitted to Sgt. Maffett. It listed items found at the scene of the accident: the bicycle, two broken pieces of glass, a damaged light assembly, a bolt, and a piece of plastic from the light assembly. Whitler stated that the glass submitted matched the fog light taken from Charles' car. The report also stated that the pieces of glass were consistent with that from a lens from an automobile assembly. Charles' fog light was missing no glass, and Ray Porter did not lean down to examine the fog light assembly. As for the glass being consistent with glass from an automobile lens, that assertion was refuted by the report submitted three months earlier by the FBI laboratory.

Maureen Bradley, FBI Agent, report October 31, 2000.

Ms. Bradley's report stated that no automotive paint was found on the bicycle, or on Dr. Sunshine's clothing. With respect to the two pieces of glass and the piece of plastic (Specimen Q1), Ms. Bradley stated, "The items in Specimen Q1 were examined visually and microscopically. With the exception of an "R" on the gray piece of plastic, there are no discernable markings present on the items to facilitate identifying their origin." At the end of the report, she stated, "Based on the examination of these items of evidence, no OEM automotive paint is present. Therefore, a make, model, and year search through the databases to the FBI laboratory cannot be conducted." The pieces of glass and the piece of plastic were the same items examined by the SLED agents, Whitler and Black.

The assertion that the glass fit "Charles' fog light" was false. Maybe it fit a damaged fog light, maybe from the wrecked 1993 Lexus, but not Charles' car.

It was interesting that FBI Agent Maureen Bradley stated on October 31, 2000 that the glass and plastic were not identifiable. SLED Agent Whitler reported on January 24, 2001 that the glass mysteriously was identifiable as automotive glass.

SLED Agent Kimberly Black's report stated that fibers on Charles' car did not match the clothing worn by Dr. Sunshine. The report also stated that a blue smear on Charles' vehicle was compared to the sneakers worn by Dr. Sunshine. She said the comparison was similar but inconclusive.

The authorities in South Carolina were creating the case as they wanted it to be, hoping to tell the media the results of "their" tests, when in fact the tests had already been conducted by the FBI three months before. The problem was that the FBI test results helped the case for Charles Outlaw, and the SC authorities would not let that be publicized.

Unknown to me at the time, the SC Highway Patrol had made a database inquiry into personal background information on John E. Brown and his brother, K. C. Brown. That information was not presented by the prosecution to Mr. Price. There was no interview of either of the Brown brothers in the discovery material submitted by Mr. Gasser to Mr. Price, a copy of which Mr. Price sent to me. There was no mention that the database inquiry on both Brown brothers was run three weeks before Charles' warrant was issued. Evidently the prosecutor chose not to reveal that Sgt. Collins knew that Charles was not the initial suspect.

Years later, I submitted a Freedom of Information request to the SC Department of Public Safety. The data I received revealed the database inquiries conducted by the authorities on the two Brown brothers. I knew that the word on the street named them from the start, and that Sgt.

Collins named them as initial suspects to Judge Davis in October 2000. Now I had the rumors confirmed, but the information was in the bottom of a file box and no one was going to know it until I made the request.

Other suspects were named and interviews conducted. That was documented in the material sent to me by Mr. Price, who got it from the Richland County Solicitor. The Richland County Solicitor would have gotten their information from the SC Highway Patrol, the Richland County Sheriff's Department (Sheriff Leon Lott) and SLED (Chief Robert Stewart). The case was such a high-profile case that the head of each of these agencies appeared at press briefings. No one was out of the loop.

FBI report showing Charles' car could not be identified

7-1a (Rev. 2-18-99)

F B I
LABORATORY

FEDERAL BUREAU OF INVESTIGATION
WASHINGTON, D. C. 20535

Report of Examination

Examiner Name:	Maureen J. Bradley, Ph.D.	Date:	October 31, 2000
Unit:	Chemistry	Phone No.:	(202) 324-4451
Case ID No.:	62D-CO-26389	Lab No.:	001004619 MA

Results of Examinations:

The items in specimen Q1 were examined visually and microscopically. With the exception of an "R" on the gray piece of plastic, there are no discernable markings present on the items to facilitate identifying their origin.

The debris submitted from scraping the victim's clothing, specimens Q3, Q4, and Q7, was examined visually and microscopically. No automotive paint was present in specimens Q4 or Q7. The white paint submitted as Q3 was further examined instrumentally by Fourier transform infrared spectroscopy (FT-IR). Based on its chemistry and lack layer structure, the Q3 paint is not consistent with an original equipment manufacturer's (OEM) automotive finish.

The victim's clothing, specimens Q8 - Q11, was examined visually and microscopically for the presence of automotive paint. No automotive paint was found on any of the clothing specimens.

The bicycle, specimen Q12, and items from the bicycle, specimen Q2 and Q5.1- Q5.2, were examined visually and microscopically for the presence of automotive paint. No automotive paint was found. The white and faint green smear present on specimen Q5.1 was examined instrumentally by FT-IR. In addition, white and green areas of the victim's sneakers (Q11.1 - Q11.2) were also analyzed by FT-IR. Based on the comparison examinations conducted, it is likely that the victim's sneakers are the source of the smear present on specimen Q5.1.

Specimen Q6, the hacksaw blade, was not examined.

Based on the examination of these items of evidence, no OEM automotive paint is present. Therefore, a make, model, and year search through the databases available to the FBI Laboratory cannot be conducted.

Chapter Seven

Charles had no way of knowing that the cards were being stacked against him. The conspiracy was in place before he was arrested and continued after he was arrested, as well as after he was released on bail in December 2000. Tshona was not released on bail. People with knowledge of the matter agreed that the authorities thought the highly excessive bail would make Charles a puppet for the prosecution. The bail was reduced to make Charles think that the authorities were on Charles' side. Charles bought none of it.

After leaving the office of Judge Finney, Laura and Charles knew something was up. No attorney goes to the jail unannounced to visit someone who never called him, does not ask for a retainer, and asks someone to perjure himself unless there is something in it for them. It's risk versus reward. But in this case the risk would be minimized because everybody involved was working toward the goal of not having a trial. The risk of exposure was minimal. The prosecutor controlled when a trial would be called. He could keep the case on the books for years, all that time harassing and threatening Charles at will. That was exactly what they did.

The next attorney Charles spoke with was Todd Rutherford. Mr. Rutherford, a young black attorney who had worked in the prosecutor's office, was now in private practice. Rutherford was also a representative in the SC House of Representatives from an urban district. Charles and Laura went to Rutherford mainly because he was black, as was the Finney family. Charles thought he could trust him.

At their first meeting, Rutherford became animated and loud, telling Charles that he knew Charles was not involved. Rutherford never told them what he knew.

Charles paid Rutherford five thousand dollars in January 2001. During the next six months Charles never had a preliminary hearing. He would call Rutherford, but Rutherford would dismiss Charles, telling him that the prosecutor assigned to the case, Johnny Gasser, and Rutherford were close friends and that he was taking care of Charles. Charles had no idea what Rutherford was doing, if anything. As was mentioned before, the only thing in Charles' file in Rutherford's office was a discovery motion and newspaper clippings. Nothing from the prosecutor was in the file.

Charles got Rutherford on the phone one time, and Laura was listening in. Charles wanted to know about his preliminary hearings. Rutherford told him not to worry about things. Rutherford told Charles that he knew that Tshona was not involved in the death of Dr. Sunshine, and that for thirty thousand dollars Rutherford would make sure nothing would happen to Tshona.

I presented the scenario to a friend of mine, an attorney. I told him that my client had not had a preliminary hearing after having been arrested six months prior. He said that Charles would have to drop Rutherford and submit a release before any attorney would represent him. Rutherford was not responding, and Charles felt stuck.

The issues that we had raised, more properly identified as contradictions, kept mounting but no attorney for Charles was going to point a finger at the establishment and make them accountable. It was as if the authorities were looking at different evidence than I had in front of me. They were presenting information to the media that was conceived in deceit. What surprised me was the fear that had been placed into the minds of all the persons associated with the prosecution; men who were afraid to confront someone and/or acknowledge that what they were doing just did not make sense. They thought no one would see what they were doing, or would confront them. They appeared to all be puppets, but the ultimate puppet master's identity was being protected.

It was earlier mentioned that when Charles bought the 1994 Lexus he found two pieces of paper in the car. One was a rental agreement; the other was a parking ticket. The rental agreement was between Hi-Line Imports and a black female named Gabrielle.

I found Gabrielle. She lived with her mother north of Columbia. She told me that she saw the 1994 Lexus at Hi-Line Imports a month before Charles bought the car. Gabrielle and her father were coming into town and the car caught her eye.

They pulled into the parking lot and Gabrielle leased the car for a couple of days. She paid Hi-Line Imports two hundred dollars to lease the car. Gabrielle thought she would want to buy the car.

Gabrielle told me that there were a number of things wrong with the car; the antenna was missing, the right fender was scratched, and the air dam under the front of the car was hanging down. All the scratches were on the passenger side of the car.

I went to Gabrielle's home and met her in person. I took the photographs I had taken at the impound facility and showed the photos to her. I wanted her to compare the condition of the 1994 Lexus at the time she drove the car with the condition of the car at the time I took the photos. The yellow stickers placed on the car by the authorities were observed in the photographs.

Gabrielle stated that the scratches on the passenger side fender, some of which were tagged with yellow Post-It®

stickers, were on the car when she test drove the car. The only scratch on the fender that was not on the car was one deep groove scratch.

As for that deep groove scratch, both Charles and Jimmy Winders told me that this damage was not on the car the day that Charles took the car to be photographed by Jimmy Winders.

Who put that scratch on the car? Was it put there by someone who wanted you to think that the scratch was the result of hitting Dr. Sunshine? When Charles first saw the car with me at the impound facility, the first thing he said was, "Look what they did to my car," and he pointed out all the scratches and the deep scratch. Jimmy Winders confirmed what Charles had told me.

Gabrielle was not the only person who saw the 1994 Lexus. Her cousin had been riding with her during the two days the car was being rented. I tracked down the cousin, showed her the photographs, and she told me the same thing that Gabrielle told me. The car was scratched and the air dam was hanging down when Gabrielle had the car.

My God I wanted a trial.

The other piece of paper was the parking ticket for the 1994 Lexus. The ticket number 50245300 was issued on the evening of August 29, 2000 at the Bethea lot on the campus of South Carolina State University. The vehicle was driven to the campus of the school, and was ticketed near the time and location of the murder of a student. The police chief, Chief White, voided the ticket four months later on January 9, 2001.

According to the conversation I had with Ms. Williams at the security office, at 11:18 a.m. on May 4, 2001, Chief White "took care of the ticket, he voided it on January 9, 2001." Ms. Williams confirmed the death of the student in the Bethea area. Chief White received the transfer of the call from me. He stated that Ms. Brown of his office was conducting an investigation, and a message was left for Lt. Edwards of SLED to contact me. Lt. Edwards returned my call, and I told him that the 1994 Lexus was parked at the scene of the murder. Edwards told me he would go to Hi-Line Imports the following day. Two days later I called Investigator Brown of the SC State University Police. I told her I had heard nothing from the SLED agent, Lt. Edwards. Investigator Brown told me that she wanted to talk to Lt. Edwards before going to Hi-Line Imports. That was the last I heard from them.

Parking tickets at colleges are not just dismissed. They add up. Students are always getting their cars towed as a result of having a ton of tickets they don't pay. In this case the ticket was dismissed, and the ticket was in Charles' name even though he did not buy the 1994 Lexus until a month later.

Why would a parking ticket here be so important that the chief of police would dismiss the ticket four months later? Who called the chief and asked him to do that?

In addition to the dismissing of the ticket, none of the law enforcement agencies investigating the murder of the student—South Carolina State University, Orangeburg City Police, Orangeburg County Sheriff's Department, and the South Carolina Law Enforcement Division—had even made the connection or investigated the matter until I brought it up to the SLED agent.

The next thing to address was Sherma and Shermica Doughty. They were the two women with Tshona at Fantasy Island.

Charles was in the office with me when I first called Sherma. Charles had the number to call. I put Sherma on the speaker, and that was the revelation to Charles that Tshona had been at Fantasy Island on the morning of September 30, 2000. I had to get a statement from Sherma.

The day after Charles was arrested (November 30, 2000) Sherma gave her statement to Tommy Robertson of SLED, Sgt. Tom Collins of the SC Highway Patrol, and Capt. Jim Stewart of the Richland County Sheriff's Department. Sgt. Collins was supposed to be the lead investigator even though three agencies were now involved in the case. It would only make sense that Sgt. Collins, whose agency arrested Charles and Tshona, would be aware of the statement given by Sharon Keels on November 1, as would Stewart and Robertson. Ms. Keels' statement identified a black Lexus from Hi-Line Imports and a black male passenger. The authorities wanted to discount Ms. Keel's account of a man being in the car and instead place Sherma in the car. They all knew the conflict but rewrote history to fit their agenda.

Ms. Keels stated she saw the "Hi-Line" Lexus at around 5:30 a.m. Ms. Keels had to be exact with the time because she was going to work. Sherma was on a time line too; she needed to be home before her boyfriend came around. Sherma was a petite black female, about 5 feet tall and weighed about 100 pounds. Her hair was short. Sherma did not look like a man.

The statement written by Capt. Stewart and signed by Sherma revealed that Sherma was home around 5:30 a.m. If Tshona dropped Sherma off and traveled south on Two Notch Road, Dr. Sunshine would have had to have been on the opposite side of the road to be struck.

Phone records would prove that, as Charles would state, Tshona called Charles on her way home to ask him if he wanted her to get him something to eat at the Waffle House. We did not know which Waffle House Tshona was referring to, but the most convenient Waffle House in that area was at the intersection of Interstate 20 and Clemson Road, the same intersection that Tshona would have passed through while taking Sherma home, nowhere near the scene of the death.

Sherma told me that the authorities went to Shermica's place of employment, Wal-Mart, to take her statement. Sherma also told me that she did not read her statement, nor did she receive a copy of the statement. Sherma stated that Richland County Sheriff's Captain Jim Stewart wrote the statement, read to her what she thought was on the statement, and asked her to sign the statement.

Sherma stated to me, "I was not told to read over the statement before signing it. I took it for granted that what was read back to me was on the paper and it was a complete statement."

Sherma was smart enough to know that the statement Captain Stewart wrote was not complete. How did we know that Sherma did not read her statement? Captain Stewart misspelled Sherma's sister's name. Neither Sherma nor Capt. Stewart corrected the spelling of Sherma's sister's name. That proved that Sherma did not read her statement, or write it.

A few days after Sherma's initial visit from the authorities, SLED Agent Reed came to her apartment again. Reed read from what seemed to be the statement Captain Stewart wrote for her. Reed was accompanied by a black male, but Sherma did not know the other man. Again, Sherma never read the statement. A few days later Reed called Sherma. Sherma told me, "He wanted me to go to the office of the Richland County Solicitor (prosecutor)." Sherma went downtown and when she arrived at the office, she was met by Johnny Gasser, the assistant solicitor assigned to the case by Solicitor Barney Giese; Sgt. Tom Collins of the SC Highway Patrol; Agent Reed; and someone else she did not know. The statement was read to her again.

Sherma told me that I was the only one to give her a copy of a statement to review, which was the statement she gave to me. Sherma was never given a copy of the statement she gave to the police.

After I received the discovery material, I gave Sherma a copy of the statement written by Captain Stewart.

Sherma told me again after reviewing the statement she gave Captain Stewart (I showed her a copy of the statement which was read to her) that Tshona did not drive up Two Notch Road in the vicinity of the accident, which was near the intersection of Two Notch Road and Polo Road. Sherma stated she and Tshona had gone to the Sports Palace before and Tshona always drove Sherma home via I-20 to the Clemson Road exit. Part of the "Complete Detail" that Captain Stewart conveniently left out of the statement he wrote was the route taken by Tshona while taking Sherma home, the fact that Sherma had two witnesses to the partial route taken by Tshona (Shermica and the cousin), and there were no geographical references in Sherma's statement with respect to "running up on something." One part of the statement Stewart wrote had Tshona and Sherma en route to the Sports Palace, but Sherma said she was feeling sick. The statement said, "We ended up going down Two Notch Road with Tshona taking me home."

Sherma was right. Captain Stewart's statement was not complete, but implied what he wanted it to say, that Tshona drove Sherma home by using Two Notch Road as far as it would take them. Stewart needed two things: He needed Tshona at the scene, and he needed her there at about 5:40 a.m.

Captain Stewart created a scenario that Tshona took Sherma home after leaving Fantasy Island, which was on Two Notch Road, and that Tshona traveled on Two Notch Road all the way to the intersection with Sparkleberry

Lane. Since Dr. Sunshine was killed a short distance before Tshona would have arrived at Sparkleberry Lane, that would put Tshona at the scene. It must not have mattered that if Tshona had taken that route at that time of night, Sharon Keels would never have seen Tshona with Sherma anyway; it was too early. The statement was incomplete. But remember that Sgt. Collins told Judge Davis while getting the warrant for the arrest of Charles that the case would never go to trial. The incomplete and misleading statements would never be put into evidence, and Sherma would never be able to give a "complete statement."

Stewart's statement had Sherma saying, "When I got out at my apartment I looked at the side and (two words which could not be read) up under it. Nothing caught my attention."

If Tshona had struck Dr. Sunshine, the vehicle would have enough damage to "catch the attention" of Sherma.

The authorities thought they had put Sherma in the car when Dr. Sunshine was killed. That would make Sherma an accessory after the fact, as well as being charged with misprision of a felony for not telling what she knew. Sherma was never arrested. Collins accused Charles of being in the car, threatening to arrest him until he learned that Charles was asleep at home. So why did Collins not arrest Sherma?

So, Sherma's route home was not clear in the "Stewart statement." The statement given by her sister, Shermica, would further complicate matters for the prosecution and contradict the "Stewart statement."

Two Notch Road would not be the route Tshona would have used. Sherma told me that Tshona had been at her home many times. Sherma had known Tshona for fifteen years. She had been out with Tshona many times, and Tshona never took her home driving on Two Notch Road;

she always drove to Interstate 20 and Clemson Road. The route would be taken that night for three reasons:

At the time Sherma announced to Tshona that she was sick and wanted to go home, she and Tshona had turned left from Two Notch Road onto Fontaine Road, then right onto Interstate

277. That road would lead them to Interstate 20, where Tshona would go west to the Sports Palace. Since Sherma got sick, Tshona would exit I-277 east onto I-20 and proceed east to the Clemson Road exit.

Sherma did not see city street lights or traffic signals en route to her home as she would have if she had traveled on Two Notch Road.

That was the faster route home, traveling on I-20.

Sherma inspected the car when she got out of the car and saw no damage. That was in the "Stewart statement." When I first interviewed Sherma she told me that the car she saw on the news was not the car that Tshona had been driving.

Collins, Stewart, and Robertson had access to Sharon Keels' statement. The time did not fit Sherma's statement, and Ms. Keels saw a man, not a woman.

How would Collins, Stewart, and Robertson make Sherma's statement implicate Tshona? The authorities used the first part of Ms. Keels' statement identifying the black Lexus observed by Ms. Keels, and then put Sherma in the car to end the story to fit their agenda. The problem with the time contradiction did not matter; the authorities were not going to trial with the case.

I then interviewed Shermica Doughty, the sister of Sherma. Shermica stated she had given a statement to SLED Agent C. R. Holloman, and Agent K. W. Reed witnessed the statement. The statement had Shermica, Tshona, Sherma, and the cousin of the sisters leaving Fantasy Island at 4:00 a.m.

If the girls left at 4:00 a.m., that would still be too soon to have been in the area where Dr. Sunshine was killed. Sherma stated she and Tshona were driving up Two Notch Road, side by side with Shermica. At a traffic light, which Shermica first thought was Parklane Road, Tshona turned left. That would take Tshona and Sherma to Interstate 20, and to the Sports Palace. When I talked with Shermica, she recounted that Tshona turned left at Parklane; she had to have turned left on Fontaine, approximately two to three miles before Parklane. Fontaine led to Interstate 20 by way of Interstate 277, and that would have been the route to go to the Sports Palace. Sherma remembered a muffler shop on the right of Two Notch Road, and it was a block or so from Fontaine.

After the SLED agents left Wal-Mart, Shermica had time to reflect about her statement. She was at work, receiving pages over the Wal-Mart loud speakers from different departments, and had trouble concentrating. Also, the SLED agents showed up with their weapons in plain sight. When Holloman took the statement, he did not give Shermica any landmarks to help her remember where Tshona turned left.

A part of Shermica's statement that the prosecution might have thought helped their case was that Shermica stated she received a call from Sherma later in the day of the accident. Sherma supposedly told Shermica that Tshona "ran up on a curb or something." Sherma said to Shermica, "…this happened somewhere on Two Notch Road," because she supposedly remembered waking up and seeing a Pizza Hut sign; then it only took a brief time for her to get home.

That statement might sound like a very damaging statement for the defense, but there were no curbs on the side of Two Notch Road in the area where Dr. Sunshine was killed. Agent Holloman must not have inspected area, and should have checked his geography before submitting a statement that would conflict with the facts. Reed was with Holloman, so neither agent from the South Carolina Law Enforcement Division knew that there were no curbs, just wide grassy shoulders, along that stretch of Two Notch Road.

Now if Holloman and Reed were going to create a statement to help implicate Tshona and the 1994 Lexus, they shot themselves in the foot by including the last sentence of Shermica's statement. The last sentence reads as follows:

"TSHONA ASKED HER (SHERMA) TO CHECK FOR DAMAGES, BUT SHE DIDN'T SEE ANY."

How about that? No damage to the car and no curb on Two Notch Road. These statements could not convict anyone.

I always wondered if the heads of the police agencies involved in the case ever knew the problems with the case, or the contradictions in the statements taken by their officers. Sheriff Leon Lott (Richland County), SLED Chief Robert Stewart, and the SC Highway Patrol were in the public eye telling everyone they had the killers. These men had a long history in law enforcement in South Carolina. Were they not privy to the evidence being "developed" under their watch? The case was to be tried by the Richland County Assistant Solicitor Johnny Gasser. Mr. Gasser had to make a case from what he was given. Mr. Gasser was under the direction of Barney Giese, an elected official.

During almost 20 years of taking statements I would interview the person giving the statement, probably on the telephone. The person would be more relaxed and could remember more. I would take notes, and create a statement from my notes. After creating the statement from the notes, a copy of a draft would be sent to the person to read and to make any corrections, additions, or deletions. That was what I did for both Sherma and Shermica.

Shermica's statement to me conflicted with the one given to Holloman. She explained that she had time to reflect. That was why I gave a person a draft to review before obtaining a signature.

My notes also included a statement from Shermica that when she got home, it was dark outside. Her fiancé was asleep on the couch. Shermica knew her clock was set to go off at 5:10 a.m. in order for her to get to work in the morning, and she would leave the house at 5:30 a.m. Shermica stated she knew she would only have one hour to sleep, so she must have gotten home around 4:10 a.m. Shermica had about fifteen minutes farther to drive than from where Sherma lived. If Sherma and Tshona changed their minds about going to the Sports Palace, as they did, turning onto Fontaine Road toward Interstate 277 would not have been out of the way; they would go that route even if they had not planned to go to the Sports Palace.

So, with all the confusion about the time everyone left Fantasy Island, and their condition, Shermica seemed less intoxicated than Sherma and recalled more detail. Shermica recanted part of her statement made to Holloman based upon further reflection. She had had no time to study what she said or to think more about the events.

Chapter Eight

Since Charles first called the office on April 30, 2001 information was coming in like a whirlwind. I had gone to Charles' house to meet with Charles and Laura. Charles and I left the house to go see Mr. Winders at Leon Jones Insurance Company, then on to my office to call Sherma. We went to see the source at Bo Jangles who knew the Brown family, went to the impound and photographed Charles' car, went to the SC Highway Department and got a history of Charles' car, went to Hi-Line Imports and met with Suhail Najjar, and prepared for the next day. That was the first day.

On May 3, I received a call from Ray Porter, met with Charles, discussed the parking ticket with SC State University officials, went back to Hi-Line Imports to get the vehicle identification number from the 1993 Lexus, and spoke again with Sherma.

Charles was constantly talking about the fact that nothing was being done for him by his attorney, Todd Rutherford. I had heard that before from many defendants, and my job would be to talk to the attorney and soothe the defendant by telling the defendant what had been done on his behalf. Charles told me on May 5 that he called Rutherford and Rutherford admitted getting a letter from Chip Price, Tshona's attorney. Mr. Price had already told me he sent the letter, but had received no paperwork or cooperation from Rutherford.

The following day I had a thirty-minute conversation with Mr. Price. As I said before, Mr. Price did not trust Charles because Charles called 911 while he and Tshona were in Atlanta. Mr. Price also told me that he had subpoenaed the coroner's office, and had filed Motion for Sanctions against Barney Giese, the Richland County

Solicitor, for not sending the complete file. Items were missing which were in the file of the SC Highway Patrol, and these items would target the original suspect, John Brown.

Later that day Charles told me that he found out he had a preliminary hearing scheduled for May 14 at 9:30 a.m. I told him I would be there and hopefully we would have more information which would get his charges dropped and help Tshona's case. In a perfect world, that is what was supposed to happen, but it did not work out that way.

At 11:38 a.m. on May 5, I called Todd Rutherford's office. The secretary, Melissa, took the call. Melissa stated that "Todd stays in contact with the Solicitor every day." She also stated that no paperwork had been received from the Solicitor (the discovery motion was filed five months before) and that "nothing will be done on the case until the court date is set"; the Solicitor has to send his file ten days before trial. Melissa further stated that "Todd did not want to push the envelope . . .Todd knows the best way to handle this . . .Todd does not know why Charles hired a private investigator to work on the case."

That conversation confirmed what Charles and Chip Price had been telling me; neither of them had received any cooperation from Todd Rutherford. Rutherford was planning to have Tshona take the heat of a trial or plea, then make some kind of bargain against Charles' will with the Solicitor for Charles instead of defending his client.

How did Rutherford plan on defending Charles with ten days of preparation? There were too many things to do. Charles had not even had a preliminary hearing. Something was wrong.

On May 8 at 12:17 p.m. I called Rutherford's office again. I was given his cell phone number, called the number, and I asked Rutherford about the preliminary hearing scheduled for May 14. Rutherford told me that he was going to reschedule the preliminary hearing, and he gave no reason. I knew Charles would explode at hearing that. When Rutherford told me that no discovery evidence had been received from the Solicitor, I suggested that I could contact the chief investigator in that office, Bill O'Neill, to get the file. Rutherford stated he would get back to me. I also told him about the matter with Sgt. Collins and the fact that Charles' car was not the car involved in the accident. Rutherford never called back.

I was helping his client, getting the truth, and Rutherford did not return calls. Charles was being told to sit tight not to raise any issues. Charles and his mother had already had the conversation with Rutherford in which Rutherford requested thirty thousand dollars to make sure nothing happened to Tshona. Laura and Charles did not trust Rutherford.

In the next two months, a lot would happen but Rutherford was never involved in assisting Charles. Rutherford sent nothing to Chip Price nor did he talk to Price about their respective clients and the crime. Rutherford did not get anything from the Solicitor because he did not ask for it. It had been five months and he had done nothing.

On May 10, I talked to Mr. Price. He told me he got a package from the Solicitor, along with a nasty letter. Tshona was still in jail, and a new bond hearing for Tshona was scheduled for May 18. I would meet with Chip and Tshona's family before the hearing. Chip said he wanted to convince Tshona's family to hire me because I had worked so hard to get information for Charles.

The following day Mr. Price's secretary told me she was sending me a copy of the discovery material sent to him by the Solicitor's office. When I told Charles, he was excited but wondered why Rutherford was not doing the same thing for him. There really was no mystery.

There was another matter I had to pursue. It involved the fact that Suhail had told Charles that Charles owed more money for the car.

On May 7, I went to First Citizens Bank. The branch that Charles had used to finance the 1994 Lexus was directly across the street from Hi-Line Imports. I told Charles that there was a discrepancy with the sale price of the car and I wanted to see the bill of sale which was sent to the bank for the financing of the car. The bank official I spoke with was Deirdre Simmons. She was very nice and helpful.

There was another problem, and it was with Suhail. The bill of sale sent to First Citizens Bank dated 9/25/00 showed a sales price for the 1994 Lexus as $16,995.00. The Buyers Order and Invoice dated 9/22/00 showed a sales price of $18,495.00. Another document dated 9/28/00 showed a sales price of $17,820.00. Something wrong was going on with Suhail and his customers and the bank. A state agency needed to get the answers, an agency which oversees the auto dealers.

Late on the afternoon of May 8, I went to the SC Highway Department. I was told that the Department of Motor Vehicles had sixteen auditing agents. The person I needed to talk to would be Mr. Roland. I was given his telephone number and I started calling and leaving messages for him.

I immediately went back to Hi-Line Imports and I saw Suhail on the lot. He walked away from me, stating he did not have anything to say to me. The following day I called Suhail and he refused to talk to me. He said I was not a friend of Charles' and that I was an investigator. I asked him the name of his attorney and he refused to tell me. Suhail was nervous.

On the morning of May 14, I went to the magistrate's office because the preliminary hearing was to take place.

Even though Mr. Rutherford said that the hearing had been postponed, Charles did not know it and he was going to see what would happen.

I went into the building and I did not see Charles. Mr. Rutherford was not there either. I saw Sgt. Collins, and he did not seem very pleased to see me. There was a lady with him who I later found out was Ms. Sunshine, the widow of Dr. Sunshine. A young male was with her, and I later found out that it was Mark Sunshine, the son of Dr. Sunshine. Rutherford was right; he had the preliminary hearing postponed. I called Laura to see where Charles was. I left before I saw Charles.

I later went to my post office box and got the discovery material from Chip Price. Now I was going to spend many hours studying the material.

Charles called me soon after I got the discovery material. He told me he went to the magistrate's office and saw Sgt. Collins. Sgt. Collins told Charles that Charles was wasting his money hiring an investigator. I assume Collins had no suggestions about how Charles was going to right the wrong that the authorities had committed against him and Tshona. All Sgt. Collins had to offer was to tell Charles to sign the statement against Tshona and life would be just fine.

On May 17, 2001, I finally got a call from Mr. Roland from the auditing office of the SC Department of Transportation. I figured that Suhail would need to answer for the fact that he had three different documents with three different sale prices, along with a wrecked 1993 Lexus on the lot. I advised Mr. Roland about the inconsistencies with the sale prices. He stated we would have to file a form MD70. Mr. Roland sounded as if I was imposing upon him, even though it was his job and his territory. He advised me that his supervisor was Billy Huckabee.

The next day Mr. Huckabee called. He stated he could not get involved until Roland finished his audit, and that he was in charge of a separate section. The audits were spot audits, using a random system. So, the automobile dealers just play the numbers and the auditing section does not investigate or audit based upon specific complaints. That was another state agency, affiliated with the SC Department of Highways and Public Transportation. Huckabee was not much help.

May 18 was to be the day of the bond hearing for Tshona. There was a faint hope that there would be a bond amount set so she could get out of jail. She had been in jail for six months, since November 29, 2000.

I met Chip Price in the lobby of the Adams Mark Hotel in downtown Columbia. When I met him, there was a contingent of Tshona's family Members with him. Tshona's mother was not there; she was en route from New York where she lived. The most vocal of the group was Sandra Lambright, Tshona's aunt, and the sister of Forcina Gaymon, Tshona's mother. Forcina was the person Laura Outlaw knew in New York. I showed them some of the documents and evidence I had compiled, including the photographs of Charles' car when it was impounded. I told them about the existence of the 1993 Lexus. Mr. Price told them, "You need to hire this man. He can help you and Tshona."

After the meeting, we walked to the court house. Most bond hearings were conducted in magistrate courts away from the main courthouse. The hearing was such a media circus that it was handled in a courtroom in the main Richland County Courthouse.

The prosecutor Barney Giese described the fact that Dr. Sunshine was left for dead on the road, and that they had all kinds of evidence against Tshona Gaymon Outlaw, along with the fact that her mother was in New York, making her a flight risk. The bond was denied.

I then agreed to meet the family at the beauty salon owned by Sandra Lambright, called NY Innovations. Sandra's mother, who was Tshona's grandmother, was there. Sandra's brother was there. (It was later learned that he was employed with SLED.) Sandra's daughter Mamchu was also there.

The family members present were:

Sandra Lambright—aunt, hairdresser Mamchu Jeff—daughter of Sandra Lambright

Dorothy Tyson—aunt, SC Department of Corrections Debra Woodard—aunt, part-time daycare worker Wylene B. John—grandmother

Sylvia—Sandra's daughter, cousin to Tshona

Unidentified male—later identified as relative employed by SLED

After I told the family about the photographs, Sgt. Collins, and the witness that test drove the car, as well as other things that would help them and Tshona, I left a contract on the table for someone in the family to be responsible and sign it.

Mamchu approached me in the kitchen located in the back of the shop. She told me that Tshona was out looking for a specific man that night. Her mother, Sandra, was getting closer to us and Mamchu acted like she did not want Sandra to hear what we were talking about.

The family was very receptive to me. A couple of the women hugged me, thanking me for helping them. Forcina showed up later. She was overwhelmed and was hugging me and crying.

Sandra did most of the talking. She stated that on the evening before the accident Tshona was at the beauty shop.

Sandra and Sylvia, Sandra's daughter, invited Tshona and Brandi to go to Appleby's Restaurant. The shop closed and the three went to Appleby's.

Sandra said that while they were at Appleby's Tshona began asking Sylvia if she was going to the party for Jermaine O'Neal at the Sheraton Hotel that night. Brandi, Tshona's daughter, went home with Debra, Tshona's aunt. Tshona went to the party by herself and was at the party from 11 p.m. until 2 a.m. Tshona then went to Fantasy Island, alone. That was where Tshona met with Sherma, Shermica, and their cousin. All three talked to Tshona in the parking lot. They were going to the Sports Palace located on Broad River Road. Tshona asked Sherma to ride with her. Sherma got sick and Tshona took her home.

My relationship with the family was very interesting. There seemed to be a rift between Tshona and Charles. The Gaymon family said Charles was controlling. Charles told me that Tshona would not stay away from her mother's family, and they liked to go to the clubs and party. Charles was less critical of Tshona's family than I thought he would be, even though Charles remembered what Sgt. Collins told us when we met with him, "Her (Tshona's) family is just a bunch of crack heads."

On May 31 Sherma called and left a message. I called her back. I had made a copy of the statement she gave to the police, along with a copy of the statement made by Shermica. I also left her a draft of a statement for our purposes.

Sherma specifically told me that she did not tell the police anything about seeing a Pizza Hut, nor did she remember saying anything to Shermica about looking up and seeing the Pizza Hut sign. She did remember a scrape, but nothing about a Pizza Hut.

Sherma said she went to the party at the Sheraton with Shermica and her cousin but did not see Tshona at the

Sheraton. Sherma went to Fantasy Island and later saw Tshona enter Fantasy Island. She thought the club closed between 4 a.m. and 4:30 a.m., but she did not know if the Sports Palace would even be open then. The police told her that the club closed later than that, but she did not think the police had even talked to anyone at the club before they talked to her. She told me they would say that just to plant something in a statement.

When she got home it was still dark outside. Tshona's headlights were on. Headlights. Plural. Neither of the headlights was broken out, like on the 1993 Lexus found at Hi-Line Imports.

On June 4, 2001, I called Sherma again. Sherma was always nice, never defensive. She knew that Tshona was in over her head and she would help if she could. I wanted to make sure the information I had on her statement was exact, but also wanted to set a precedent for the route taken by Tshona to Sherma's apartment. Sherma told me she had been at the Sports Palace with Tshona four or five times over the past year or so before the accident. The last time was a birthday party in March of that year, and they got home that night between 3 and 4 a.m.

I still needed to track down the 1993 Lexus to determine if Suhail was lying about the damage. I had been to a Lexus dealer in Columbia before, asking about the fog light assembly so I went back on a lark. One of the clerks, Bobbi Brazell, got the service record online for the 1993 Lexus. I had no way of knowing that, but I just had to keep firing questions at Bobbi. Bobbi printed out the service record on the vehicle; the last time it was serviced it was registered in the name of Kenneth Woodard, in Romeoville, Illinois.

I had to go find my man in Romeoville. The telephone number for Woodard on the service order was wrong. That was no shocking surprise.

The following day I went north of Columbia to meet with Gabrielle, who had test driven Charles' Lexus a month before Charles got the car. I gave her a draft of a statement for her, and one for her cousin. I had already given her a set of the photographs to review at her leisure. No pressure was on her. I wanted them to review the statements and make sure everything was complete. I was not going to approach them and demand a statement on the spot by trying to intimidate them.

Later in the same day I got the statement from Shermica. She had called me and said the draft was correct and complete. She asked that I come to Wal-Mart to have it signed. I went to Wal-Mart, gave her a copy of the statement, and returned with my copy.

By June 5 Charles had become a very restless soul. There were so many issues involved, and many people too. The charge against him was a misdemeanor, but the police do not go two hundred miles to another state to arrest someone on a misdemeanor unless there is something else going on. Also, a person's bond for a misdemeanor is not $250,000. People were trying to get Charles to lie. His attorney did not want him to defend himself by hiring a private investigator. So, Charles started making calls to hire a different attorney to get a preliminary hearing.

I could not let one day go by without making follow-up calls on the case. It was an everyday matter. Charles would call me every day.

Kenneth Woodard, who had owned the 1993 Lexus, was not necessarily hard to find, but he was not listed in the databases. It was a challenge, but the job was not finding him; the job was finding someone who knew him. So, on Saturday June 9, 2000 I telephoned a number which I had generated and thought it might be Kenneth's mother. A young lady named Shana answered the phone. Shana told me that her mother had gotten out of the hospital that day because of having a stroke. Shana said, "Kenny is hard to get up with. Give me ten minutes and call me back." I did not know if he would call because Kenny did not know who I was and he might be running from something or someone.

In the meantime, I made more calls.

The phone rang and it was Ray Porter on the phone. Ray was the auto body repairman who worked for Larry Aaron, and who Charles spoke with during his only visit to Aaron's Body Shop. I was trying to address the two statements he had given the police without making him feel like he had been duped by them, which he had. I just wanted him to know that I would let him review anything I wrote, and would let him read it before he signed anything.

I take good notes. Years after the call from Ray, my notes speak volumes about the statements obtained by the police versus the truth. I knew Ray personally. I had sold him a car. He got a good deal and knew I was not out to take advantage of him. The authorities came to him heavy handed. He did what he had to do to get them to leave him alone.

I doubt that Ray would call the authorities on his own just to discuss the case or his statement.

Ray told me the following:

The authorities asked him to profess an opinion about the damage to Charles' car although he told the authorities he had never given an estimate before.

Ray never got down on the ground to inspect the fog light. (The fog light could not be inspected because it was recessed under the bumper.) He was trying to keep the customer, so he didn't want to seem anxious.

The authorities first came to the shop looking for a white Lexus; they returned looking for a black Lexus.

Don't Get Arrested in South Carolina

The man that returned to the shop a few days after seeing Ray on Saturday seemed to be the same guy, but the man did not have gold teeth. (That eliminated Charles.)

I would spend Saturday afternoon working on Ray's statement. There were issues to be addressed in Ray's statement; these included the female who was with the black males that went to the shop on different occasions, the woman in the second car (there was not a woman in another car when Charles was there), the authorities taking one statement from Ray, the authorities coming back to get another statement from Ray and asking him to give an estimate (which he was not qualified to do), the authorities getting a statement from Larry which did not have an estimate figure on it, plus a comparison of the statements.

The statements taken by the authorities had issues to be addressed and rebutted, but their agenda was to get a person to sign the statement and let them know that if the matter goes to trial, the statement would be read to them and they would be in trouble if they recanted. Ray was one of two people from whom two statements were taken. The cops had to go back and take another statement because the first statement did not say what they needed it to say. In Ray's case, the first statement was taken by a member of the SC Highway Patrol, Roger Hughes, and a SLED agent, C. Gregg Shockley. The second statement was taken by two SLED agents, Reed and Holloman. The comparison was shocking. Agent Shockley was the agent who took the statement from Suhail Najjar on December 1, 2000, a month after the initial Ray Porter statement. And guess who took the statement from Sharon Keels? It was Roger Hughes of the SC Highway Patrol.

The case was beginning to sound like All the President's Men, except we were not sure who the president was. I was looking for a Deep Throat.

Ray's first statement, taken by LCpl Roger Hughes of the SC Highway Patrol and SLED Agent Shockley included the following excerpts:

"driving a "newbie" model Lexus"

"damage to right front fender, bumper, and post along windshield, also passenger door, scuff marks and other damage"

"customer wanted an estimate on the damage"

"I could not help him because my boss does the estimates"

The top of the form stated he only had completed the 11th grade

After Ray made that part of the statement, a horizontal line was drawn under the wording. The statement started up again, which was something I had never seen before, and was a bit creative. Patrolman Hughes and the accompanying officer who witnessed the statement (whose signature was not legible) must have decided to add information to the statement.

"Damage I observed to vehicle was damage to the fog light in bumper with glass missing, damage to top right fender along with damage to post and top of door green and white marks. In my opinion, the damage was done by something other than a vehicle."

I am going to assume that the officers had more formal education than Ray, but the last sentence of the statement left a lingering question: If Ray thought the damage was done by something "other than a vehicle," why did the authorities not ask him to identify what he thought did the damage? That was a very curious way to end a statement.

With respect to the second statement, taken twelve days later by SLED agents Reed and Holloman.

Ray Porter was now listed as a high school graduate. The SLED agents, Reed and Holloman, had added another year of education to Mr. Porter's background, or maybe he graduated between the time of the last statement and the date of this statement.

There was no mention in this statement of any missing glass.

"The vehicle had damage to the right front bumper, the right front fender, right front door, and the windshield door post. (Charles' car did not have that damage).

The word "subject" was used to describe the black male who Ray saw on Saturday, September 30. That word was not in the vocabulary of Ray Porter. It appears SLED Agent Reed wrote the statement, and to his own specifications.

"The subject further stated that the damage occurred when he was parked in a parking lot. However, it was not consistent with what I believe it should be if hit in a parking lot." He, being Charles, was not parked in a parking lot. Tshona was parked in a parking lot. Also, "if hit in a parking lot" with or by what? A truck? A rock? A meteor? These guys would be fodder on the witness stand for even a marginal attorney.

Ray gave an estimate of damage between $1,000.00 and $2,000.000. First of all, not only was Ray not authorized to give an estimate (see his first statement above), he refused to make an estimate both to Charles Outlaw on September 30 and to Patrolman Hughes on November 1. SLED Agents Reed and Holloman not only conferred a high school diploma upon Ray, they qualified him by asking his opinion of the damage.

The only reason SLED Agents Reed and Holloman went back was because they needed evidence to get probable cause for a warrant for Charles and Tshona. The police were screaming about the fact that they had evidence at the scene of the accident; glass on the ground (which was discounted by the FBI), a piece of plastic, and a Lexus vanity plate. Plus, they had a statement from Sharon Keels stating that she saw a black Lexus. Sgt. Collins had seen the wrecked 1993 black Lexus at Hi-Line on October 20 but no one did forensics on that vehicle. (Sgt. Collins ultimately did not include those photos in the permanent record reviewed by me in 2004). The fact was that SLED officials sent Reed and Holloman to Ray Porter to obtain a statement which was not credible but served their purpose. You would think that they would be privy to the original statement so as not to appear unprepared. They were not, and did not think anyone would figure it out. They were told what to do and what to get, but who was ultimately directing them?

Chapter Nine

The statements obtained by the three police agencies were inconsistent in many ways; evidently the men in the field were not privy to statements taken by other officers, nor did they understand that the statements they were taking were conflicting with other statements. They discounted information which exonerated Charles, and if the account of events did not fit the crime as they wanted, they would make it fit. That was true with Sherma Doughty and Ray Porter.

Larry Aaron's statement revealed that he had sixteen years of schooling, so I assumed that meant he had a college degree. Larry was wise, smart, and crafty. He would say exactly what he was thinking. For instance, Larry said to me, "I told the police they were dumb asses," after he explained to the police that clear coat paint transfers as a white color on a car, not the color of the car. Larry was well connected in the legal community and had a devil-may-care attitude. It was good to see someone who could not be victimized or intimidated by a badge.

SLED Agents Reed and Holloman took Larry's statement. The statement was very vague. There was no description of the black male who approached Larry at Aaron's Body Shop. Did the police ask, or did they care? Larry's statement did not have a written estimate of the damage Larry observed. Larry owned the business. Larry was the boss. Ray even said so in his first statement. Ray also said that he, Ray, was not authorized to give an estimate. Larry was the only one authorized to give an estimate. The estimate was the basis of the charge of having damages in excess of one thousand dollars. So, since Sherma could not estimate the damage, Suhail did not remember the damage, and Larry did not give an estimate, all they had was Ray.

So why did Agents Reed and Holloman not put an estimate in Larry's statement? Maybe Larry told the SLED agents what he told me; that he did not give the man in the black car an estimate on his damages. Larry said he only walked around the car briskly, plus the man to whom Larry was talking did not have gold teeth in the front of his mouth. Charles had prominent gold teeth.

It did not matter about the validity of a statement; Sgt. Collins had already told Judge Davis that there was not going to be a trial. All he wanted was the arrest of the man whose picture was on his wall; he wanted to arrest Charles Outlaw, and to get his hands-on Charles' car.

Look at the time the statements of Ray and Larry were given. Both were given on November 13, 2000. Ray gave his statement, including the unauthorized estimate, at 3:10 p.m. Larry gave his statement, minus an estimate of damages, at 3:40 p.m., thirty minutes later. Agent Reed wrote Ray's statement; Agent Holloman wrote Larry's statement. I never learned if Larry knew that Ray had given an estimate to the authorities.

The authorities also had two statements from another witness, James Brown. Mr. Brown was the man who witnessed Charles and Tshona arguing across the street from his workplace on Main Street. This argument occurred on Saturday, September 30, 2000, only a few hours after Dr. Sunshine was found dead on Two Notch Road.

The first question was, "Where did James E. Brown emerge as a witness to anything?" Unless the authorities, or someone, had been watching Charles at that time, there was no way the authorities would know about Mr. Brown. James Brown's statement was given before Charles was arrested. Charles did not tell Sgt. Collins about Mr. Brown before Charles was arrested. In a subsequent interview, Mr. Brown never told me he called the authorities. So, the authorities got a statement from Mr. Brown before his existence was revealed by Charles.

The first statement was given by Mr. Brown was on November 25, 2000, four days before the arrest of Charles Outlaw. The statement was taken by an officer from the SC Highway Patrol. It appeared to be given in the presence of Cpl. S. D. Brildas (I could not read his handwriting). The officer's signature was not legible.

Mr. Brown stated that he had looked at the damaged 1994 Lexus and said the fog light was cracked and half the lens was missing. That was the first time that had been stated. One would think that if Larry or Ray had noticed that half the lens was missing they would have mentioned it. That was a huge discrepancy. Ray and Larry noticed things like that in their line of work.

If Tshona hit a curb, as she had indicated, the next sentence would be interesting.

"Right front passenger rim was scratched."

Well, there were no curbs on Two Notch Road in the vicinity where Dr. Sunshine was killed. Rims get scratched by curbs, not by grass.

After Charles and Tshona argued, Charles left and walked the one block to Hi-Line Imports. Tshona used the telephone offered by Mr. Brown, and her aunt arrived driving a blue Mazda.

She arrived in a blue Mazda about fifteen minutes later." "She" was Tshona's aunt, Sandra Lambright.

Tshona did not leave with Sandra. Sandra left the area after Charles returned from Hi-Line Imports; then Charles and Tshona left the area.

Don't Get Arrested in South Carolina

The second statement given by Mr. Brown, dated December 5, 2000, was ten days after the first statement. This second statement was taken by SLED Agents Reed and Shockley. Agents Reed and Holloman took the second Ray Porter statement as well as the statement from Larry Aaron. Did Agents Reed and Shockley review previously taken statements to make sure the content was what they wanted, then go re-interview the witnesses and get the additional information they were assigned to get? Both Ray Porter and James Brown gave two statements.

Why did the authorities need to take two statements?

The second statement referred to Mr. Brown having seen Charles and Tshona arguing. According to Mr. Brown, Tshona said, "Supreme (Charles' nickname), I'm sorry I wrecked the car. I hit a ditch or a curb." Again, as in the first statement, "One half the fog light was missing."

"There was damage above and below the fog light, damages as in scratches and dents. There also were scratch marks going up onto the hood of the car."

Reed and Shockley made sure to put that in there since it was in the first statement. But they made fatal flaws.

"There was also damage on the front right quarter panel above the tire; damage as in scratches and dents. There were also scratches and dents on the front right tire rim."

Again, there were no curbs or ditches in that area of Two Notch Road. The police wrote there were more scratches on the wheel rim. Again, grass does not scratch metal rims.

"The black female (Tshona) asked me if she could use my phone to call a family member. I let her use my phone. About an hour later the family member showed up. They all talked for about a minute or so. Then the family member, a black female, left by herself."

If they were going to quote the fact that one half the fog light was missing, you would think they would get it right when they thought it took an hour versus fifteen minutes for Sandra to arrive in the previous statement.

"When I (James E. Brown Jr.) was looking at the damage I did not see any mud, dirt, or grass on the car to show it had been in a ditch. The car was clean."

Of course, the car was clean. The car never left the asphalt.

I had written hundreds of statements. The difference was that my statements were evidence in court proceedings. These statements would never make it into court. That was not why the statements in this case were taken. They were designed to intimidate weak defendants to show them that the authorities had stacked the deck against them, so they had better know who the boss was.

Laura and Charles were not buying it, and the authorities knew I was not either. The Solicitor, Barney Giese knew we wanted a trial. I had told Bill O'Neill, the chief investigator, just that. Bill did not know at the time we had the test driver in our pocket, but cross examining the SLED agents who wrote the statements would be embarrassing to them and Chief Stewart. Plus, they knew that the case was a very high-profile case, and hopefully media from outside South Carolina would be there to see it. And Bill O'Neill, who I could talk to directly, knew I was not going away.

On Sunday, June 10, 2001, I was back at the office. The two things I wanted to get done were to find Kenneth Woodard and finish the statement with Ray. The hardest part of getting my own statement from Ray was to let him see the two conflicting statements he gave to the police; I was not going to hide anything from him. He would learn that the authorities, who included the SC Highway Patrol and the South Carolina Law Enforcement Division, were playing him and Ray did not want to do anything to confront the police. I had pointed some things out to him and I could tell that he was getting a little defensive and scared. Ray did not have the formal education that the authorities supposedly had, and they used their authority to write these statements for him, knowing Ray would not question the contents.

About 10:30 a.m. I called Shana in Illinois. I was still trying to find her brother Kenneth, who previously owned the 1993 Lexus. I was encouraged that on the previous day she told me she would try to find him for me. When I called her, a man answered the telephone. I did not realize the number I was dialing was a cell telephone number. I left a message with the man, Shana's boyfriend, for Kenneth to call me.

Right after that I called Ray Porter. He agreed to come to my office later that morning.

Ray came to the office at 11:25 a.m. He told me he could come in at that time so I did not put him off. Even though I knew Ray, I knew he would still be a bit nervous around me concerning the case because the police seemed to intimidate him. Ray was not the type to be able to get on the witness stand and make a very convincing argument if he was not telling what the authorities told him to say.

I was impressed that Ray came to the office on a Sunday morning. I showed Ray the photographs that I had taken of Charles' car while it was impounded. I took notes as I let Ray look at the photographs, and we talked. I told him I would type up the statement and get a copy to him to read before signing anything. There was no pressure on him. In the first part of the statement it was stated that he was approached by a SLED agent named Roger Hughes. That was my mistake; Hughes was employed with the SC Highway Patrol. Agent Shockley was with Hughes, and Shockley's name can be found as the witness on that statement. The following is the text of the statement I wrote as a result of my interviews with Ray:

"I, Lester Ray Porter, 22 years of age, married, residing at 211 Arbor Drive, Columbia, SC, and being employed with Stiver's Chrysler Jeep, Lexington, SC in the body repair shop, do state the following: On November 1, 2000, I was approached by a SLED agent named Roger K. Hughes while I was at work. At that time I was working at Aaron's Auto Body Shop, which is located at 121 Calvin Drive, Columbia, South Carolina. In my statement of that day, I stated that a black male came into the shop about four weeks prior to the arrival of Mr. Hughes. The male was driving a black Lexus, which had damage to the right front fender, the bumper, the post along the windshield, the passenger door, scuff marks, and other damage. The male asked for an estimate on the damage. As I told Mr. Hughes, the owner of the shop does all the estimates, I fix the cars. I took a name and pager number from the man and gave the number to Larry Aaron. I made no notes and did not lean down to look as the lower part of the car. If there was glass missing from the top region of the fog lamp I would never have seen it. As I approached the car I looked at the fog light and noticed that glass was missing on the left side of the light. Glass was still in the light fixture on the right side because the mounting screw was still in the fog lamp assembly, which kept the right side of the glass from falling out. The amount of glass missing was about ½ to ¾ of the bottom of the glass, not just a small piece. November 13, 2000, almost two weeks later, I was approached again by SLED agents Reed and Holloman to give another statement. The statement I gave agents Reed and Holloman, of which I have received a copy from J.B. Simms, states that the damage on the Lexus was the right front bumper, the right front fender, the right front door, and the windshield post. I was asked during the second statement to estimate the damage to the car. I was not asked this question during the interview for the first statement. I did give the SLED agents an estimate because they asked me to, but I have never given an estimate for cost of repair while I was employed by Larry Aaron. Some parts of the damage probably could have been repaired rather than replaced, and it sometimes costs a lot more to replace than to repair. Agent Reed wrote the statement and put on the statement the part about my estimation of the damage. As I stated in the first statement, I do not give estimates, have never taken a class in estimation. During the second visit, I was shown a photo lineup and was asked to pick out the man that brought the Lexus to the shop. I could not identify him. I did speak with the man, face to face, but I did not remember him having a gold covered front tooth. I have been shown a group of photographs by J.B. Simms, private investigator. The photographs appear to be the Lexus I saw, but the fender of the one I saw had a crease which I could not see in the photograph. The door post had a bend in it, which I did not see in the photographs. The gouge mark in the bumper seen in the photographs was not on the Lexus when I saw the car."

Ray was one confused and scared person.

The points to be made from the statement Ray Porter made were these:

- He made no notes and did not lean down to examine the car.
- If glass was missing from the top region of the light, as the police alleged, Ray would not have seen it. Ray did not get on his knees. Ray goes on to describe missing glass.
- Ray did not give an estimate to the man in the Lexus.
- The owner (Larry Aaron) gave all the estimates.

- Ray never gave an estimate while working for Larry Aaron, but the SLED agents wanted him to give one, without qualification.
- Ray had never taken a class in estimation.
- Ray was face to face with the man in the Lexus. Ray did not remember gold teeth in the front of the man's mouth. Reed and Holloman showed Ray a line-up. Ray could not pick out the man in the Lexus from the line-up. Contradiction.
- Ray thought that the pictures I showed him of the 1994 Lexus was the one brought in, but he could not identify anyone in the photo line-up.
- Damages listed by Ray in his statements to the SLED agents were not present on the vehicle in the photographs of Charles' 1994 Lexus. The vehicle had not been repaired. Contradiction.

After I typed up the statement, I noticed that there was a notation, "cn id girl" on the officer's notes, which meant that Ray could not identify the girl accompanying Charles. That must have been the same identification lineup card used to try to get Sharon Keels to identify Tshona, the one which she could not identify Tshona either. There were between nine and twelve photographs. Ms. Keels did not identify Tshona on the lineup (and the police conveniently left that out of Ms. Keels' statement) and Ray could not identify either Charles or Tshona.

I got the statement ready and called Ray a day or so later. I told his wife that I would bring the statement over to the house. I told her he could read it and get back to me. The statement had to be what he wanted, and it had to be the truth. There were major contradictions in the statements submitted by agents Reed and Holloman of the South Carolina Law Enforcement Division. I left the draft of the statement, seen above, with his wife.

Ray had told me that his wife's father was active in the small-town politics in the area where they lived, located adjacent to Columbia. Apparently, her father had held some elective or appointed post. Ray's wife and her father were not pleased that Ray got involved. The fact that Ray would come to my office on a Sunday morning and talk with me showed that he trusted me, as he should have. But when he saw the photographs of Charles' car and looked at the statements written by the SLED agents Reed and Holloman, he knew what they had done to him.

I made a few calls to Ray over the next week. There was no big hurry. Finally, I got Ray on the phone and asked him about the statement. Ray told me that the statement was fine, but that his wife and father-in-law did not want him to get involved anymore. They would not let Ray sign the statement, even though he told me it was correct. Ray had a wife and an infant, and must have been scared. Ray never signed it. Clearly, Ray was now being controlled by his family.

Later on the same Sunday that Ray came to my office, I called back to Illinois to see if I could talk with Ken Woodard. At 6:30 p.m. I called Ken's sister again. Her boyfriend answered the phone again. The boyfriend told me that he did not know where Ken was. He thought he was out of town.

Thirty minutes later I got Ken' sister Shana on the phone. Shana told me that Ken was in a bar at that moment. She gave me the telephone number for Ken's pager, so I called the pager number and left my telephone number.

The person I was trying to talk to was in a bar in Illinois, who I assumed was going to call me back because I paged him? I paged him at 7:08 p.m. but I did not wait up for a return call that night. The following day I was back at the Lexus dealership asking questions. I thanked Bobbi for helping me and amused her with the story about the previous owner of the 1993 Lexus. Bobbi directed me to the parts window, where I talked to a young woman named Laurie. I asked her one of the most important questions in the entire investigation: Do the 1993 Lexus GS300 and the 1994 Lexus GS300 have the same fog light assembly? Laurie told me that the parts from the years 1993 through 1997 were all interchangeable, including the clips and brackets, fog lamps, and headlights. The fog light would need to be replaced as a unit.

Laurie had no idea how important that information was. Charles' car was at the impound facility. The fog light assembly had been removed. There was no chain of custody or evidence of the removal of the light in the discovery material. The 1993 Lexus admittedly had been observed by the authorities and documented by photographs before Charles' warrant was issued.

The authorities had statements from the following persons:

- Sharon Keels, October 25, 2000, taken by LCpl. Roger K. Hughes, SCHP
- Ray Porter, November 1, 2000, taken by LCpl. Hughes (SCHP) and SLED Agent Shockley
- Ray Porter, November 13, 2000, taken by SLED agents Reed and Holloman
- Larry Aaron, November 13, 2000, taken by SLED agents Reed and Holloman
- James E. Brown, November 25, 2000, LCpl. S. D. Bridas (SCHP), not notarized
- Sherma Doughty, November 30, 2000, taken by James T. Stewart, Richland County Sheriff's Department; Thomas Collins, SCHP; and Tommy Robertson, SLED.

- Suhail Najjar, December 1, 2000, taken by SLED Agent Shockley (not notarized; no witness)
- James Winders, December 1, 2000, taken by SLED Agent Holloman
- James E. Brown, December 5, 2000, taken by SLED agents Reed and Holloman
- Shermica Doughty, December 7, 2000, taken by SLED agents Reed and Holloman

Suhail Najjar did not give a statement until December 1, 2000. Charles had already been arrested and transported back to Columbia, and would be out of jail in a few days. Sgt. Collins had been at Hi-Line Imports on October 20, 2000 photographing the 1993 Lexus. Sharon Keels would not be interviewed and give a statement until October 25, 2000.

Evidently Suhail had a convenient memory problem. His written statement for SLED Agent Gregg Shockley did not mention the wrecked 1993 Lexus which had been damaged, but that Charles Outlaw bought the 1994 Lexus on September 27, 2000. Charles returned a few days later without the car (having walked the block from the temporary work area where James Brown was) and told Suhail that his girlfriend had an accident, and Charles wanted the car fixed. Suhail then stated that Charles returned with the car, and after examining the car, Suhail stated, "I don't recall where the damage was."

Everybody else remembered damage; some remembered more than others, and some remembered damage on Charles' Lexus that did not exist. Suhail remembered nothing, and SLED Agent Shockley let it go at that. Shockley did not notarize the statement, and did not give a copy to Suhail. They knew they would never use it.

Chapter Ten

The next week was filled with talking to Charles, Laura, and Sandra Lambright; working on Ray Porter's statement; trying to get Ken Woodard to return calls; and studying the discovery materials.

The 1993 Lexus was repaired somewhere. Since Suhail did not like me anymore because he had been deceived about my identity, I knew he would not tell me where the vehicle had been repaired. He had all the repair information on his computer. Maybe he had someone do it onsite. Who knew?

I went back to Lexus of Columbia and talked to Laurie Cox again in the maintenance area. She was going to research repair orders from Hi-Line Imports. The result was that Hi-Line Imports had not purchased any parts matching the ones necessary to repair the 1993 Lexus.

I had some business with an attorney who was sharing space with an attorney named Greg Stoudemire. I did not know Mr. Stoudemire, but I was told that Suhail had hired Mr. Stoudemire. I left a message for Greg to call me.

The lady working for me in my office called me on the afternoon of Wednesday, June 13, 2000. Ken Woodard had called the office and she took the call. Ken told her that he bought the 1993 Lexus from The Auto Barn in Evanston, Illinois in either 1995 or 1996. Ken financed the vehicle through VW Credit. He moved to New Orleans, and the vehicle was repossessed in New Orleans. Ken also stated that the 1993 Lexus had no prior damage when he bought it, and was not damaged while he owned it.

If I could find the 1993 Lexus entering South Carolina, undamaged, Suhail would have more questions to answer, as would Sgt. Collins.

On the following day, I had a long discussion with Chip Price. Chip had no respect for the Solicitor's office in Columbia (Richland County) or for Johnny Gasser. We discussed the route Tshona took to take Sherma home, Charles not testifying in Tshona's trial or just pleading the Fifth because of his pending charges, plus the fact that I had sent photos of the car off to a specialist. Chip was filing a Motion to Compel to have Barney Giese, the elected Solicitor, release the information that was being withheld. Chip wanted to have a meeting with me within the week.

We got through to VW Credit to find the origin of the 1993 Lexus.

It was learned that the vehicle was repossessed, then sold on April 13, 2000 to Westside Imports, located in Mableton, Georgia. It was later sold through an auction in Atlanta. I could not get an answer at Westside Imports.

While I was waiting to get information about the 1993 Lexus, other things had to be done. I drove to the home of the cousin of Gabrielle to obtain the statement from her about the condition of the 1994 Lexus, Charles' car, when it was being rented/test driven. I had left photographs with Gabrielle for her and her cousin to study before giving any statement. Her cousin was very nice and helpful to me. She agreed that the air dam was hanging down and that the scratches on the vehicle were there when they test drove the car.

After I got back I wrote a letter to Sgt. Collins to ask for an explanation of the denial of the existence of the 1993 Lexus. I knew that it might be an exercise in futility, but if and or when the case went to trial, he would have to account for the fact he ignored the letter. I faxed it to him. Sgt. Collins did not reply.

Friday, June 15, was the day I was going to go see Tshona. Tshona was being housed at the Richland County

Detention Center in Columbia. The detention center had since changed the name to honor a slain guard, Alvin S. Glenn. I had interviewed many persons in many different prisons and jails; some were clients, some were witnesses, and some were sources. But this was not a prison; this was a jail where persons stay for a sentence of a year or less, or are being held until their trial.

When I arrived, I was told by a female officer, Sgt. Friedley, that I would have no personal contact with Tshona. I would have to communicate with her from behind a glass. I could not exchange any documents with her. She could not write any notes to me. I questioned this new procedure and Sgt. Friedley referred me to a captain who I believe was named Renfroe. Neither would acknowledge that her family had retained me to interview her and authorize the legal visit. I had been in that jail countless times and had documents to be signed, documents to receive, and personal exchanges, but had never been denied contact with a prisoner before this.

Tshona came into the booth. I had to talk to her through a speaker box. She seemed very shy, but pleasant. I told her who I was. She told me she knew my name from her family members. I drew a map of the area of Fantasy Island, Two Notch Road, Fontaine Road, and Interstate 20. Since I could not exchange paper with her, I had to hold the paper up on the glass for her to see. I asked her to tell me which direction she went home. Tshona told me that she took Sherma home as my map indicated, from Two Notch Road, left onto Fontaine, right onto I-277, right onto I-20, exit I-20 at the Clemson Road exit, Exit 80. I then drew a diagram of the Clemson Road exit, showing that as Tshona would have exited at Clemson Road, turning left, she could have under steered the vehicle and scraped the fencer and wheels on the curb. She said that was possible. She stated that she went with Charles on the Saturday morning after the accident to Hi-Line Imports, and also to Aaron's Body Shop.

Tshona told me that she did not know what time she left the club. She did leave with Sherma in her car; then Sherma wanted to go straight home. As for the air dam hanging down, she said it was that way when the car was purchased. I could not talk to her in those restrictive conditions. It was ridiculous. I did ask her if she killed Dr. Sunshine. She said no, and she told me she would submit to a polygraph. That was a start.

I left and was going to try to do what I could to get to talk to her personally. That never happened.

I cannot overstate how frustrating it was to try to talk into a little box, and there was no privacy there. People were standing around behind me and could hear every word I said.

Chapter Eleven

The same day I went to see Tshona in jail I received information that the 1993 Lexus had been sold from Westside Imports in Atlanta. The owner of Westside Imports was Chuck Moore. I obtained a telephone number which was said to be Chuck Moore's number, and I left my number for Chuck to call me. I was still tracking down the ownership of the 1993 Lexus, plus, I was going to dispel the story that Suhail was telling that the 1993 Lexus was wrecked when he bought the car.

On the following Monday, June 18, I called Chip Price and advised him of my visit with Tshona. I told Mr. Price the visit did not seem to be very productive, but the fact that she agreed to a polygraph was a good start. I knew a couple of polygraph examiners and I knew we could get her in quickly. I also mentioned to Mr. Price about Sgt. Collins's and other police activity relating to a cover-up of information about the 1993 Lexus, as well as the charges against Charles.

The original charge against Charles was, as was typed on his arrest warrant number G638281, dated November 17, 2000, was FAILURE TO REPORT CERTAIN ACCIDENTS. The offense code was 56-05-1270. The offense needed to be researched to see the actual penalty for the misdemeanor.

I went to the Richland County Courthouse to look at the file of the arrest of Charles. Nothing was in the file except for the Motion for Discovery filed on January 31, 2001 by Todd Rutherford. I talked to a clerk, who looked up the penalty for the charge against Charles. She told me that the charge against Charles was an "unclassified misdemeanor," which the statutes did not provide a penalty for, and that the most Charles could be sentenced would be thirty days, which would be the penalty for an unclassified misdemeanor. She then referred me to the SC Court Administration office for further research and clarification.

The South Carolina Court Administration office was the place to get the definitive answer about the charges and if Charles had a chance to challenge the charges. I met with Terry Leverette. Terry fit the profile of the clerk having gray hair, glasses, and being the studious type. Terry was very nice and accommodating and did not seem to be bothered by my questions.

Terry told me that the charge against Charles, 56-05-1270, was an incorrect charge. The charge, noting the last four digits of the code violation (1270), was a charge against a person who was involved in an accident, a person who was at the scene, "involved" in the accident. If Sgt. Collins was going to charge Charles with a crime, assuming the car that hit Dr. Sunshine was Charles' car, the code violation would be 56-05- 1270. The last four digits, 1230, referred to failure to give information about an accident if the police were not called, and the accident resulted in bodily injury, death, or damage in excess of $1,000.00. The bottom line was that Mr. Leverette did not find a definitive penalty for these misdemeanors, but he stated that an unclassified misdemeanor had a penalty of $500.00 and/or thirty days in jail.

So, Sgt. Collins had charged Charles with the wrong crime. Either way, the penalty for either "crime" did not fit the bond placed upon Charles after he was arrested.

The original bond for Charles was $250,000.00. The bond was reduced to $25,000.00. This was an unclassified misdemeanor charge, and the maximum fine would be $500.00 and/or 30 days in jail. What a joke.

I learned later that the prosecutor's office used the same warrant number, G638281, and placed the charge of Hit and Run on the screening sheet in the Clerk of Court. Hit and Run was a major felony. The authorities knew Charles was not in the car because they had put Sherma in the car to replace the unidentified black male. And if Charles was being charged with Hit and Run, why was Sherma not charged as an accessory after the fact? Who did Sherma know to keep it from happening?

The day would not be over yet.

Charles kept telling me that he had not had a preliminary hearing. Mr. Rutherford had filed the Motion for Discovery on January 31. No evidence had been received from the prosecution. I decided to pursue the issue of the preliminary hearings.

I called the court administrator and was told that I needed to talk to Ms. Dorch. Ultimately, Ms. Dorch's account of the matter of the preliminary hearings and Sgt. Collins was more than I expected.

Ms. Dorch told me that five different preliminary hearings had been scheduled for Charles; all had been continued by the State. The dates of the scheduled hearings were as follows:

- February 16, 2001
- 2. April 2, 2001
- 3. April 9, 2001
- 4. May 14, 2001
- 5. June 12, 2001
- 6. July 6, 2001 (to be canceled per Sgt. Collins)

All these hearings had been scheduled by the court, but according to Ms. Dorch, "All parties agreed to all the postponements. Mr. Rutherford has not objected to any continuance."

Ms. Dorch stated that sometimes the prosecutor and the defense attorney got together and postponed those hearings.

She further stated that the reason no additional hearings had been scheduled was due to Sgt. Collins.

After one of the last scheduled preliminary hearings, Sgt. Collins called the clerk's office and he was very rude to the lady clerk. Ms. Dorch used "annoyed" as the word used by Collins to the clerk. Ms. Dorch stated that during that call, Sgt. Collins told the clerk that he did not like wasting his time coming down for these scheduled preliminary hearings. Sgt. Collins stated emphatically that ". . . the preliminary hearings will be continued indefinitely."

Ms. Dorch did not have another date scheduled. She stated to me, "I do not have a dog in that fight."

Who was taking orders from whom? Was Sgt. Collins telling the prosecutor when to have the preliminary hearing? What would be the reason for postponing it six times? The obvious reason was that the prosecution did not want the general public to know the truth about the trumped-up charges against Charles. The general public would only know the "facts" as presented by the media, and the media got their information from the authorities and the prosecution, so the authorities controlled the truth. The media in central South Carolina refused to print anything about the story which would question the integrity of the authorities.

I called Charles and left a message. I knew that the revelation about the preliminary hearings would set him off, but I kept nothing from him. When Charles called me back, he was trying to get another attorney.

It was important to find the origin of the 1993 Lexus and prove that Suhail lied. Collins had to have known Suhail lied and did nothing about it to make Suhail accountable.

I finally got Chuck on the phone. Chuck was the owner of Westside Imports. It had been days of waiting for calls, leaving messages, and I needed that information now. Chuck was receptive. He told me he sold the 1993 Lexus on May 2, 2000 to Speedway Imports in Atlanta. I phoned Speedway Imports, Bishop Brothers Auction, the Georgia Used Car Board, Bishop Brothers again, and then the Atlanta Auto Auction.

BINGO. I finally found someone who could understand what I was trying to do. I talked to Sherry at the Atlanta Auto Auction. She was a Godsend. She told me that Suhail Najjar, of Hi-Line Imports, bought the 1993 Lexus on June 21, 2000. Hi-Line Imports had a dealer number registered with the Atlanta Auto Auction. A minor flaw on the vehicle was negotiated, but the body was not damaged. The car had not been wrecked, and was not sold as wrecked. Sherry had received no calls about the car since it was sold. No police had called. That was no surprise, but I had to ask.

I could prove that Hi-Line owned the 1993 Lexus on June 21, 2000, three months before the death of Dr. Sunshine and that it was not wrecked when it was purchased. Suhail had lied about the 1993 Lexus having been in the wrecked condition when he bought it. If Sgt. Collins had wanted to confirm that the vehicle was wrecked when it was purchased, he could have done the research I did and arrested Suhail for the same charge as Charles. Suhail did not have an accident report to substantiate the damage, and Collins did not ask. No one was going to challenge Sgt. Collins except me, and Collins was not the big fish.

The charge against Charles alleged there was more than one thousand dollars of damage to Charles' car as a result of the "death of Dr. Sunshine." The lower air dam had already been damaged and was hanging loose, and the person who test drove the car attested to the scrapes on the car prior to Charles owning the car. The only damage that Tshona caused was the scrape on the bumper and the cracked fog light lens. The light was not broken, and according to Charles the light still worked, despite the fact that the lens was cracked diagonally.

After calling the local Lexus dealership, I was referred to a toll-free number for Lexus to find out some specifications on the 1994 GS 300 model. I was told that the body style of the GS 300 was the same from 1993 through 1997. The parts were interchangeable. There was a wholesale change in 1998. The minimum ground clearance for that model was 5.5 inches or 140 millimeters. That was very low. That low clearance would allow that model to scrape a very low barrier or curb.

I was told that a repair manual would be helpful to price out repair costs.

The people at the Lexus dealership told me that they had used John Harris Body Shop to do repairs to their Lexus automobiles. I called John Harris Body Shop and talked to Jim McCorkle. Jim told me, as did the others, that the 1993 through 1997 models were the same. The service manual for the GS 300 would illustrate areas of the vehicle, and the specification sheet would show the cost of the parts.

I went to see Jim McCorkle the next day, June 20, 2001. I showed Jim the photographs of Charles' car that I took at the SC Highway Patrol impound. Jim gave me the specification sheet on the damaged area. Jim told me that the bumper for the Lexus was a three-piece item: the metal bumper, a foam absorber, and the bumper cover. Since the bumper cover on Charles' car was just scraped, it could be buffed or if it had been creased, it could be heated and pushed out. Either way, the retail cost of the bumper cover was three hundred dollars. The cracked lens cover for the fog light occurred as a result of the scrape and the torque of the lower part of the front assembly. The assembly surrounding the fog light was not damaged; the protruding bumper kept the underside of the car from being damaged.

Replacing the bumper cover and fog light lens would all be necessary replacements to repair the car. The paint scratches were on the car when Charles bought it but the police did not know that. It was not one thousand dollars' worth of damage, and now we could prove it. Collins knew that, but who was going to challenge Collins, especially since he was the one determining when Charles was to have a preliminary hearing? We would have to challenge him outside the courtroom and dare them to give Charles a trial, which was exactly what we did.

During the first part of Sgt, Collins's "investigation," a number of persons had been interviewed. The information was in the discovery material Mr. Price had sent me. There were statements from persons who had heard rumors. Some owned Lexus cars that the authorities inspected. If they had been as diligent in pursuing Suhail and the wrecked 1993 Lexus as they were in going to people's houses and taking statements, the matter would have been over with quickly. The authorities even impounded one man's car. No record of any interview with John Brown, his brother K.C, Duane Everett, or any former employees of Ampro were discovered.

Over the next few weeks I reviewed the "fluff" in the file. I was still calling Ray Porter, communicating with Chip Price, and talking to Charles about Rutherford and Sgt. Collins. During that time, I received a call from Mr. Stoudemire, the attorney for Suhail. Suhail told Mr. Stoudemire that he did not want to give a statement, and that I could pick up the photographs I left at Stoudemire's office.

On July 6, 2001, I met with Chip Price in his office in Greenville, South Carolina. Chip told me that Tshona had said she had nothing to do with the death of Dr. Sunshine. Mr. Price wanted to know the identity of the previous owner of Charles' vehicle, if Sharon Keels clocked in on the morning of the accident, and he also wanted me to talk to someone at Fantasy Island about Tshona and Sherma.

A few days later, on July 9, 2001, I talked with Laura. She told me that Charles had an appointment to meet with another attorney on the next day. Laura also told me that Charles had just gotten a notice for a preliminary hearing which was scheduled for July 13.

When Charles called me back we discussed the case and then discussed the ultimate insult. While Charles' vehicle was being housed in the SC Highway Patrol impound facility, Charles had to continue to make the payments on the car to First Citizens Bank, and to continue to pay the annual taxes on the vehicle.

After obtaining the vehicle history on Charles' 1994 Lexus, I saw that the vehicle was previously owned by Bradley Motors in Austell, Georgia. I called their office and talked to Bill. Bill told me that he remembered the car. The car had high mileage and therefore it would be difficult to finance the car. Bill remembered that he sold the car through an auction, but he did not remember which one. He bought the car at an auction, and sold it through an auction. He gave me the name of Adesa Auction to call.

I called Adesa Auction. They found the record of the 1994 Lexus. Their records showed that there was no condition report available, but the vehicle did show some type of damage. The 1994 Lexus was sold to Bradley Motors on June 14, 2000, and the vehicle had 95,702 miles on it.

I was hoping to get Sherry at Atlanta Auto Auction on the phone since I had spoken to her before. I called Atlanta Auto Auction and asked for Sherry. I ended up talking to someone else, who, after I gave her the identification information on the car, including Hi-Line Import information, told me she could only talk to the buyer or seller of the 1994 Lexus. She told me that I would need a court order to get more information.

Charles' 1994 Lexus and the 1993 Lexus came from the same place. That was convenient.

Just before calling the Atlanta Auto Auction, I called the post office located at the corner of Alpine Road and Two Notch Road in Columbia. The time was 12:30 p.m. and I was hoping that Sharon Keels was not at lunch. When I called and asked for Ms. Keels, she came to the phone. I told her who I was and asked her if she clocked in on the morning of September 30. Ms. Keels told me that she was a supervisor, and she said that she did not clock in or use a time sheet.

The next day, June 10, I was on the phone almost all day. I called Charles, Fantasy Island, and Sandra Lambright; faxed copies of the vehicle origination to an attorney in Atlanta that Chip Price had associated on the case; and then called Laura.

Laura told me that Todd Rutherford had called and wanted to talk to Charles. Charles told his mother, Laura, to tell Rutherford that he was getting a new attorney, that he did not want to talk to Rutherford, and that Charles "was burned out with the whole thing."

Charles came to my office the next day to draft a letter releasing Rutherford as his attorney. Charles wanted me to take the letter personally to Rutherford's office. Charles signed the letter, and I took it to Rutherford's office. I left my card and the letter from Charles with the secretary, Melissa, to give to Mr. Rutherford. The time was 4:55 p.m. on June 11, 2001.

Neither I nor Charles would hear from Rutherford until July 18, 2001.

Case Procedure Record for Charles Outlaw's case

Case Detail   Page 1 of 2

Richland County Public Index Search

NEW SEARCH | COUNTY HOME PAGE

Case Number: G638281	Court/Agency: Central Court	Filed Date: 12/02/2000
Case Type: Criminal-B	Case Subtype: General Session Mag	
Status: Disposed	Issuing Judge: Clerk Of Court	Disposition Judge: Hudnall, Clevette L
Disposition: Transferred (S)	Finalized: 08/03/2001	
Disposition Date: 08/03/2001	Date Received:	Arrest Date: 12/01/2000
Law Enf. Case: G638281	True Bill Date:	No-Bill Date:
Prosecutor:	Indictment Number:	Waiver Date:
Case:		
Probation Case:		

Parties

Name	Race	Sex	Party Type Description	Active/Inactive
Bolt, J Dennis			Attorney	A
Collins, T. B.			Officer	A
Outlaw, Charles M	Black	M	Defendant	A
Rutherford, J. Todd			Attorney	I

Actions

Filed / Begin Date	Name	Description	Completion Date
02/16/2001	Outlaw, Charles M	PRELIMINARY HEARING	
02/16/2001	Outlaw, Charles M	CONTINUED FOR THE STATE FROM PRELIM	
04/02/2001	Outlaw, Charles M	PRELIMINARY HEARING	
04/02/2001	Outlaw, Charles M	CONTINUED	
04/02/2001	Outlaw, Charles M	CONTINUED FOR THE STATE FROM PRELIM	
04/09/2001	Outlaw, Charles M	PRELIMINARY HEARING	
04/09/2001	Outlaw, Charles M	CONTINUED FOR THE STATE FROM PRELIM	
05/14/2001	Outlaw, Charles M	PRELIMINARY HEARING	
05/14/2001	Outlaw, Charles M	CONTINUED	
06/12/2001	Outlaw, Charles M	PRELIMINARY HEARING	
06/12/2001	Outlaw, Charles M	CONTINUED FOR THE STATE FROM PRELIM	
07/13/2001	Outlaw, Charles M	PRELIMINARY HEARING	
07/13/2001	Outlaw, Charles M	CONTINUED FOR THE STATE FROM PRELIM	
08/03/2001	Outlaw, Charles M	PRELIMINARY HEARING	

http://www4.rcgov.us/PublicIndexSS/CaseDetail.aspx?CaseNumber=G638281   7/27/2006

Chapter Twelve

Charles had been trying to get work during the time after he was arrested. He had worked as a detailer at a major car dealership, but since his picture had been in the newspaper and on television, people had been recognizing him and he had difficulty getting work. The money paid to the attorney, Todd Rutherford, and the money paid for the bail, was a combination of money borrowed from Happy (Laura's cousin), Laura, and other family members. Since Charles could not find work, he and Laura were struggling.

Rutherford, who never challenged the postponement of any preliminary hearings for his client Charles, wanted to meet with Charles. He was the same person who took five thousand dollars from Charles, obtained no discovery evidence from the prosecution, and objected to Charles hiring a private investigator to impeach the testimony of the arresting officers as well as the investigators assigned to the case.

Laura and Charles both told me that Rutherford attempted to get an additional thirty thousand dollars from them; he said that if Charles paid him the thirty thousand dollars, he would make sure nothing happened to Tshona.

Charles wanted nothing to do with Rutherford.

After taking the letter from Charles to Rutherford's office on July 11, I had not received a call from Rutherford. The letter, signed by Charles, requested that Rutherford give me the file. We knew it was empty, but Charles needed to confirm that nothing had been done on his case.

At 4:00 p.m. on July 18, I went into Rutherford's office. The receptionist/secretary, Melissa, refused to release the file. I asked for Mr. Rutherford. I was announced, and entered Mr. Rutherford's office.

Mr. Rutherford refused to release the file or acknowledge the letter I delivered for Charles. Mr. Rutherford told me he would need a power of attorney from Charles for me to get the file.

Rutherford was going to get what he asked for.

Charles came by my office the next day. I drafted the specific Power of Attorney, signed by Charles, which authorized me to obtain all documents in the possession of Todd Rutherford. I wrote a cover letter to be attached to the Power of Attorney. At 3:00 p.m. on July 19 I delivered the letter and the power of attorney to Melissa at Todd Rutherford's office.

On July 23 Charles called me at 10:00 a.m. Charles told me that he was quite sure he was being followed. When Charles would call me, he would jump from subject to subject, so I had to pay attention to what he was saying. He gave me a description of the vehicle he saw following him. Laura had told me the same thing before; she had been followed too. Charles also told me that he never asked Todd Rutherford to postpone any preliminary hearing, and that Charles did not know that was happening until I told him. Charles then complained that Rutherford wanted Charles to ". . . shell out 30G and Tshona would be all right." Charles was furious and felt betrayed.

I went to Rutherford's office at 4:00 p.m. Melissa told me the file was not ready.

I then went to Fantasy Island, the club where Tshona supposedly met Sherma. I talked to a doorman named Sean. Sean told me that the police had been by Fantasy Island and Sean was shown a line-up with faces of black women. Sean identified Tshona, but he did not remember seeing her on the morning of September 30, 2000. Sean stated he told the police that he did not remember what time the club closed that night. There was nothing written down, and all the time sheets had been thrown away. He told me that he had seen Tshona in the club a lot.

Charles and Laura did not know that Tshona had been going out with her friends to clubs after leaving Brandi with either Charles or Laura. On the night before Dr. Sunshine was killed, Tshona left Brandi with her cousin Debra.

When I returned to my office from Fantasy Island, I called Todd Rutherford and reached him on his cell phone. Charles had given me the number. Rutherford refused to release Charles file, stating that he "did not know me" (his bosses in the Solicitor's office as well as the chief investigator had been dealing with me for years). Rutherford refused to acknowledge the Power of Attorney he requested.

The conversation was direct, and loud. Rutherford accused me of yelling at him. Maybe I did, maybe not.

Rutherford was telling me that he had been in constant contact with the prosecutor, even though Rutherford's file was empty. Rutherford said, "Johnny (Gasser) is a personal friend of mine. I can go to his house anytime and eat with him. They (the prosecution) need to know that he (Charles) is not on his wife's team. If he has a preliminary hearing, Johnny will come back with a charge of accessory (after the fact) and can make a presentment to the grand jury with other charges."

The following are excerpts of the conversation I had with Mr. Rutherford:

Rutherford: I am not doubting your credibility. What I am telling you is, have his new lawyer call me. If he does not have a new lawyer, he needs to get one RIGHT NOW. Once I notify the Solicitor's office that I don't represent him, he's going to be in trouble if he does not have a lawyer. But if you know those people in the Solicitor's office, then you ought to know that.

Simms: Johnny (Gasser) knows me very well.

Rutherford: Tell Mr. Outlaw that if he has no lawyer, he's going to be in trouble. He needs a lawyer RIGHT NOW. There is no reason why he has fired a lawyer (acknowledging the letter delivered by me signed by Mr. Outlaw on the previous day) or, according to you, fired a lawyer, and he does not have a new one. That makes no sound legal sense, and if that is the advice you are giving him then you are giving him bad advice. He's not in a position to be. . . without a lawyer. It is going to hurt him. I told him they don't want him, and I told him he is not the target of the investigation. If he doesn't believe that, that's fine. But if he is out there without a lawyer, it is totally a different ball game.

Simms: Well, there is a prelim coming up in a couple of weeks . . .

Rutherford: No, there will be no prelim until I say there is a prelim. If you are friends with Johnny Gasser, he would have told you that. Johnny, Knox, B.A. (Elizabeth Levy's nickname), everyone in that office and myself have been in constant contact, weekly contact, about this case. Everybody knows what the deal is. But he does not, and nobody can communicate with him or you because you are not with the team; you know that. And so, without a lawyer, he is going to get screwed.

Simms: You have echoed the same thing that Sgt. Collins said; they don't want him.

Rutherford: Exactly, and that is what my point to him is. If he goes through and he is firing me, and he is doing all sort of stuff that looks crazy, then this is a different ball game. Because the fact that they don't want him does not

mean that they can't get him on some trumped up bullshit.
You know that. And the second he looks unstable, the
second he looks like he is going out there ranting and
raving about what they are doing, they have a reason to talk
to him. They have no reason to believe that he is part of
their team; there is no reason to believe anything except for
the fact that now they can mess with him. He has no
lawyer; he has nobody protecting him, and even if he gets a
lawyer. . ..

Simms: . . . that lawyer might not be able to cut the same
deal you could.

Rutherford: Exactly. Exactly. I mean I have worked in
that office. I've been in that office. I know all those folks,
and you know I have personal communication with Johnny,
O'Neill, B.A. (Elizabeth Levy), Knox, and on a weekly
basis about this case.

Simms: Are they (Charles and Laura) supposed to trust
what Johnny (Gasser) says?

Rutherford: The thing is this: all they want, all they want
is his wife. Okay? And I have talked to the person
(garbled). As long as they can get her, that is the ball game.
Nobody is looking at Charles for anything. And that charge
they got against him now is bullshit. And even Accessory
after the Fact is bullshit. But it is also something that he
doesn't need.

As I was digesting that amazing conversation with Mr.
Rutherford I received a telephone call from Harold A.
Smith, who used to work for Hi-Line Imports. Mr. Smith
did the paperwork for Charles when Charles bought the
1994 Lexus. Mr. Smith told me he remembered Charles
buying the 1994 Lexus, as well as the scratches that were
on the car when Charles bought the car. The 1994 Lexus
has been on the lot only a brief time before Charles bought
the car. Mr. Smith remembered that the 1994 Lexus had

been rented to the black girl for the weekend prior to Charles buying the car.

Harold told me that the 1993 Lexus arrived on the lot in June 2000. The accident was September 30, 2000. A man came, put three thousand dollars down on the car, and brought it back wrecked. The man had put eighteen-inch chrome rims ("fancy rims" as described by Sharon Keels) on the car. Customers would come in and borrow cars all the time and there should have been a record of these people.

Charles called my office at 3:40 p.m. the next day. He said he had talked to Rutherford. Charles said, "Todd is lying about everything. He told me he did not want to embarrass the solicitor by having a preliminary hearing. There will be too many news cameras there."

Charles told Rutherford that Sgt. Collins wanted to place other charges against Charles. Rutherford said, "Fuck Sgt. Collins." Rutherford refused to talk to the other defense attorney, Chip Price. Rutherford also told Charles that if he got a preliminary hearing, the Solicitor would put additional charges against him. How did Rutherford know that?

Rutherford agreed to give up Charles' file on the following Friday.

On the morning of July 26, 2001, Laura had a conversation with Rutherford. Laura asked about Charles getting a preliminary hearing.

Laura taped the call.

Rutherford: There is no reason to get a date. There is no reason to push anything. The Solicitor in this state calls the case. The Solicitor in this state is responsible for bringing cases to trial. If the Solicitor wants your case to sit for three years, your case sits for three years. And if you push it, and if you push it and nobody wanted you anyway, all of a sudden somebody finds a way to come after you because you made them look bad, as opposed to just sitting tight and letting them take care of you. I am telling you, whoever is giving him that advice has no idea what they are talking about. I worked with those people and talked to them every day. I talk to the Solicitor.

Laura: But Todd, first of all, the warrant is no good.

Rutherford: It doesn't matter. This charge here they have him on is nothing. There is no way they can prove the charge. But this does not keep them from re-arresting him for other things, or making his life hell, and they have prosecutorial immunity. You can't come after them, and all they are saying is "Todd, just tell your boy, just tell him to sit tight, have him sit tight. We'll take care of it; just have him sit tight." What I am telling you is, if they think the impression . . . to them that you are trying to buck them . . .

Laura: No.

Rutherford: . . . but that is how it is going to come across. Why do you need a court date? We told you we were going to take care of you. Who is going to take care of Charles?

Laura: Let me ask you one other question. What about Sgt. Collins putting another charge in the computer. What gives him that authority?

Rutherford: Sgt. Collins does not have that authority. Charles does not have another charge. Sgt Collins is nothing; he is not an elected official, and he is not over the highway patrol. He is simply somebody that works down there that doesn't like Charles. But you know what? It doesn't matter, it doesn't matter. No, he has the same charges he was arrested on.

This was the end of the conversation. Clearly, Rutherford knew things that he was not willing to share with his client.

Rutherford agreed to give up the file so Charles could get a different attorney. Charles picked up the file on Friday, June 27, 2001. The only thing in the file folder was newspaper clippings, a copy of the request for information from the prosecutor which had been filed over six months prior, and a copy of the warrant. There was no information in the file from the prosecutor.

Rutherford had been retained by Charles. Chip Price had been retained by Tshona. Chip Price had sent me a huge file of information he had requested from the Solicitor. Rutherford had sent me nothing.

Charles knew it and he wanted his money back because of Rutherford's actions, or lack thereof.

Chapter Thirteen

I never knew when Charles would call me. And as I said before, I never knew who he had talked to, and to whom I would have to explain his gregarious nature.

There were so many complex issues in the case. When Charles started talking, he talked so fast and hit so many issues that people unfamiliar with the case would become confused. Charles thought that people were just not listening. I felt the same way at times, but things had to be done in some kind of order. Charles was harping on the evidence noted by the authorities about the shards of glass, plus the fact that the FBI report revealed, three months before the SLED report, that the shards of glass at the scene could not be identified as originating from Charles' car, or any car. That was one of many issues.

I was in the office on Sunday, June 29. At 4:00 p.m. Charles called me. Charles told me he had called the FBI and told them about the activity of the state authorities in this case. Charles wanted to press charges against them for a civil rights violation. Charles told me he talked to Special Agent Dave Espie, just five minutes before he called me. I was wondering why Charles was bothering these people on Sunday. Charles had been victimized by the police, attorneys, and prosecutors. He wanted someone to listen to him, even on a Sunday. So, I called Agent Espie after Charles hung up.

Special Agent Espie was very gracious. He told me that Charles had been calling him (unknown to me, or anyone else) and that Charles wanted an appointment to talk with the FBI about the corruption in local law enforcement and the prosecutor's office.

Mr. Espie told me he was the "go between" between SLED and the FBI concerning the death of Dr. Sunshine.

Mr. Espie also stated, ". . . the FBI office was not happy with the SLED investigation." Mr. Espie had helped run down leads for SLED on this case. He told me that the SLED report showed that white "stuff" on the Sunshine bicycle was from a vehicle. Mr. Espie said that was not true. "The white stuff on the bicycle was road debris, not paint or from a shoe."

Mr. Espie also told me he saw Dr. Sunshine's bicycle at SLED headquarters. He stated that neither the women in the lab, nor the technician named David Black, "were qualified"; they "did not have the expertise to say that 'about the white stuff'" or to draw any conclusions about forensic matters. In conclusion, Mr. Black was "totally out of line."

Mr. Espie was aware of the FBI lab results which came from FBI headquarters. I mentioned to him that the SLED results, submitted three months later, contradicted the FBI results. He was indignant that SLED would try to exclude an FBI report. That probably explained the fact that upon my receipt of the SLED case file after filing a Freedom of Information request, the FBI lab results were not in the SLED file.

Two days later, on July 31, 2001, Harold Smith met Charles and me in a restaurant near my office. Harold worked at Hi-Line Imports at the time of the death of Dr. Sunshine. Harold was a tall black man, about the same height as Charles. Harold mentioned the names of other persons who worked there at the time who would know about the 1993 Lexus and Charles' car. He also told me that Charles' 1994 Lexus had factory rims, not the fancy rims described by Sharon Keels, the postal worker. Harold left Hi-Line a few months after the death of Dr. Sunshine. It was evident that Harold and others knew more than they wanted to say. They did not want to be on a witness stand. They were scared.

Charles told me he had been calling the television stations trying to get some attention drawn to what the prosecution was doing, and the fact that his car was not involved in the death of Dr. Sunshine. He had already been told by friends and others that the car shown on television after Charles was arrested was not Charles' car. The authorities had the best of both worlds; they had Charles' car, they had access to the wrecked 1993 Lexus, and they denied its existence even though we saw the photographs.

Charles hired Dennis Bolt to represent him as his new attorney. I met with Charles, Laura, and Dennis at Dennis' office. Dennis had been a defense attorney for many years. I had been involved in many criminal defense matters with Dennis. I worked closely with him a few years earlier on a case in which a "moonshiner" had been arrested with three hundred gallons of illegal liquor at his property. The defendant had testified in court that he was being extorted by a law enforcement official, and the defendant had given the officer a total of twenty-eight thousand dollars in bribes. My client was found not guilty. The officer who was given the twenty-eight thousand dollars was now working for the South Carolina Law Enforcement Division, SLED. Evidently SLED had some very interesting hiring practices.

Mr. Bolt had agreed to pursue the preliminary hearing for Charles. Charles wanted media attention at the hearing, so he called a newspaper writer from The State, the local daily newspaper. Kimanthia Lewis, a local reporter, met with Mr. Bolt, Charles, Laura, and me from 4 p.m. until 5:30 p.m. on August 1, 2001. Ms. Lewis was to write the story, but the story made little difference. The newspaper had already printed Charles' photograph as well as the story given by the authorities. No one really cared as long as someone went to jail.

The next day I spoke with a television reporter named Ainsley Earhardt, who worked for WLTX television in Columbia. Charles had been calling Ms. Earhardt and wanted her to see his car. She could not get into the impound facility, so I furnished her the photographs I had taken in May for her to examine. Ms. Earhardt and her cameraman Mike Remia came to Charles' house and interviewed Charles, Laura, and me. The story was aired later that day. Ms. Earhardt had the photographs to show on air, and I distinctly remember her telling me, "This car did not hit anyone."

She interviewed the three of us on air. Ms. Outlaw and Charles both expressed their concern for the Sunshine family. I pointed out the photographs and the lack of damage to Charles' car.

Over the next week, I spent a lot of time preparing documents and making notes for Mr. Bolt to use at the preliminary hearing. It was scheduled for the following week. We would be ready.

Chapter Fourteen

I had given Mr. Bolt a copy of the statute noting the charge against Charles. The charge, Failure to Report Certain Accident, had no penalty. I told Mr. Bolt about my interview with Mr. Leverette, and supplied Mr. Bolt with that information. That was done for Mr. Bolt because time was of the essence and he knew I would cover all the bases for him.

Mr. Bolt argued that the charge against Charles was nothing more than an administrative charge from the highway department, similar to a traffic ticket. Furthermore, the prosecution did not get a written estimate of the damages. They talked to a twenty-two-year-old high school dropout (Ray Porter), who was unauthorized to give an estimate; Sherma Doughty, who saw no damage; and Suhail Najjar, who did not remember any damage. Sgt. Collins never saw the car before getting the warrant.

The preliminary hearing was conducted at the beginning of August 2001. The hearing was conducted in a small magistrate's courtroom. We assumed that Charles' charges would not be dropped, but we did know that if we could expose a bit of the corruption it would help in the long run. I wanted to see how desperate the prosecution would be to get to Charles.

The courtroom was full. Television cameras lined the side walls. Mr. Gasser put Sgt. Tom Collins on the witness stand. There would be no testimony from the defense. The hearing would be held for a judge to decide if there was enough evidence, whether credible or not, to continue to charge the defendant and have a trial.

Sgt. Collins testified about the witness, Sharon Keels, who saw the black Lexus on Two Notch Road as she was going to work on the morning of September 30, 2000. Sgt.

Collins failed to tell the courtroom that Ms. Keels failed to identify Tshona as being the driver of the car or that there was a black man in the passenger seat.

Sgt. Collins told the courtroom that Charles had called 911 from Georgia during Thanksgiving weekend of 2000. There were two calls made by Charles and the police communications in Georgia could find only one for us. Charles acknowledged to us that he called 911 because Sgt. Collins had continued to call him, and because Tshona never admitted anything to Charles. Charles called 911 and told the operator that the authorities had accused his wife of being involved in a death, and that she and her mother were leaving. Charles was trying to keep Tshona and Forcina from leaving. Charles was helping Sgt. Collins, but Sgt. Collins made it sound like Charles was involved in some kind of cover up or was trying to escape arrest.

The basis of the warrant against Charles was the statement given by Ray Porter. The authorities made two trips to get an unauthorized estimate of damages from Ray.

The date of the warrant was November 16, 2000.

James E. Brown, who saw Charles and Tshona talking to the police officer on the morning of September 30, did not sign a statement until November 25, 2000. Agent Reed of SLED went back to Mr. Brown to get another statement on December 5, 2000. Ray Porter's second statement, again taken by Agent Reed, was taken November 13, 2000. The only person who Sgt. Collins could use for probable cause for arresting Charles would be Ray Porter.

Sgt. Collins, who had been sitting with the Sunshine family during the hearing, was telling the courtroom that he had witnesses who would state that the 1994 Lexus had damage exceeding one thousand dollars.

I wondered who they were; if not Ray Porter, Larry Aaron, Sherma Doughty, Suhail Najjar, or James Brown, then who? Evidently the judge believed him. The language of the narrative on the warrant was as follows:

The defendant, Charles M. Outlaw, who is the registered owner of one 1994 Lexus GS400, licensed 290 LPL; VIN # JTAJS47E8R00787755; did commit the crime of Failure to Report Certain Accidents in that on September 30, 2000, the Lexus was involved in a collision. No report of this accident has been filed with the department to date. The damage was over one thousand dollars. Affiant and others are witnesses to prove same.

This warrant was signed November 16, 2000 by "Thomas B. Collins" and the judge who signed the warrant was Michael Davis.

The first thing about the narrative was that the model number of the vehicle was incorrect. The correct model number was GS300, not GS400, but the most damaging part of the narrative was the last sentence, "Affiant and others are witnesses to prove same." The affiant was Sgt. Thomas B. Collins. Sgt. Collins was not a witness to the vehicle because he had never seen the vehicle. So, in polite terms, Sgt. Collins misrepresented the facts to a judge in order to get the warrant, and to another judge at the preliminary hearing.

Mr. Bolt did an excellent job explaining to the judge and the courtroom that the charge was administrative, not a criminal act. The judge shuffled her papers while Mr. Bolt talked and never made eye contact with Mr. Bolt. She was not focusing on Mr. Bolt. The judge held the matter over for trial.

When we came out of the courtroom the media were interviewing Mr. Gasser and Mr. Bolt. Sgt. Collins was standing with the Sunshine family. Laura and Charles were standing with me. Laura told me that she wanted so badly to express her sorrow for the death of Dr. Sunshine directly to the family, not because of Charles, but because Laura was that kind of person.

I heard that Mr. Gasser and Mr. Giese were not pleased that Charles finally got his preliminary hearing, nor were they pleased about our television interview. That would be evident when, on August 17, 2001, less than two weeks after the preliminary hearing, Sgt. Collins testified before a grand jury to have Charles indicted for Accessory after the Fact, which was a felony. Sgt. Collins was the only witness for the state. The indictment was signed by Warren B. (Barney) Giese, the prosecutor of Richland County.

Charles was not told of the additional charges until months later. That was their little secret.

Todd Rutherford was right. The preliminary hearing would offend the prosecution to the point that Barney Giese, the solicitor/prosecutor, would allow, or direct, Sgt. Collins to address a grand jury, and state that Charles Outlaw:

"did in Richland County between September 30, 2000, thru November 29, 2000, knowing of the commission and completion of the felony, Reckless Homicide and/or Leaving the Scene of Personal Injury, Accident, Death, by the principal felon, Tshona Gaymon, aid, harbor, and assist such felon to escape detection or arrest or otherwise avoid the consequences of the crime."

My head was spinning. Charles did not get his car fixed. Charles was hiding nothing. Charles reported the damage to a police officer (witnessed by James E. Brown) and the officer told him that the damage was so minimal that he need not report it to the highway department. Charles reported the damage to his insurance company a few days later. Charles called 911 twice to have Sgt. Collins look at the car and to interview Tshona. Sgt. Collins tried to get Charles to say that Tshona told him she was involved in the death of Dr. Sunshine. Sgt. Collins told Laura Outlaw that he was sending Charles a lawyer, and that lawyer, Jerry Finney, tried to get Charles to lie and say that Tshona told him she was involved. Former SC Supreme Chief Justice Ernest Finney also tried to get Charles to give a false statement. Tshona had given no statement, and had not told anyone that she told Charles she committed any crime. Charles refused to lie for anyone.

Charles kept telling people he was not going to lie. So, Sgt. Collins and Solicitor Barney Giese had Charles indicted with a felony because Charles tried to expose them on television. Rutherford was right.

Sometime later an interesting document was discovered in the file at the clerk of court. A screening sheet was in a file, noting the defendant, a direct presentment or warrant number, and the charge. The warrant number on the screening sheet for Charles, G638281, which was the same warrant number for the charge of Failing to Report Certain Accidents, had now been changed to Hit and Run. How do you change a charge with the same warrant number from an unclassified misdemeanor to a felony? After the initial accusation by Sgt. Collins that Charles was the passenger in the car that hit Dr. Sunshine, Sgt. Collins found out and knew that Charles was home asleep at the time of the accident, regardless if Tshona were involved. Hit and Run? Charles was going to be charged with a felony? The solicitor's office had changed the charge against Charles and kept the same warrant number.

The person who should have been having the preliminary hearing was Sherma Doughty. I had nothing against Sherma, but there was no explanation why Sherma was not charged. The fact was that she could and should have been charged. Sherma could have been charged with misprision of a felony for not telling the police that Tshona hit Dr. Sunshine, as the authorities were alleging. Sherma also stated she saw no damage on the vehicle. Maybe Sherma was not in the vehicle which struck Dr. Sunshine.

Sharon Keels' statement put a black male passenger in the vehicle at 5:30 a.m. between five to eight minutes from the scene. Based upon all statements given by Sherma, she was home before 5:00 a.m. Shermica was not as drunk as Sherma, and she stated she left the club at 4:00 a.m. If that was so, then Sherma was probably home no later than 4:30 a.m. Either way, the police used the part of Ms. Keels' statement that suited them, removed the black male from the vehicle, put Sherma in the vehicle, and assumed that Tshona must have been driving at ten miles an hour, or less, to be observed by Ms. Keels at 5:30 a.m.

J.B. Simms

False Indictment against Charles Outlaw: Accessory after the Fact

STATE OF SOUTH CAROLINA)   INDICTMENT
)
COUNTY OF RICHLAND   )

At a Court of General Sessions, convened on August 17, 2001 the Grand Jurors of Richland County present upon their oath:

ACCESSORY AFTER THE FACT

That Charles Outlaw did in Richland County between September 30, 2000 thru November 29, 2000, knowing of the commission and completion of the felony, Reckless Homicide (§56-5-2910) and/or Leaving Scene of Personal Injury Accident-Death (§56-5-1210(A)(3), by the principal felon Tshona Gaymon, aid, harbor, and assist such felon to escape detection or arrest or otherwise avoid the consequences of the crime.

Against the peace and dignity of the State, and contrary to the statute in such case made and provided.

Chapter Fifteen

Following the preliminary hearing for Charles, and the additional charge of Accessory after the Fact, the next few months involved getting the tapes from Georgia, getting all our statements signed, and hoping that we would be able to have a private conversation with Tshona.

I had been keeping Tshona's family informed of my work, but I started having a sinking feeling. I felt they knew information that they were not telling me.

I made calls to the Gaymon family from time to time. I needed to collect money from them. I never got the entire retainer from them. One day I went to the grandmother's house and was given a check for partial payment. I trusted them. That was a mistake. They turned on me.

Chip Price told me that it looked like Tshona was going to take a plea. We were shocked. That did not affect Charles other than the fact that he would not have to testify against his wife. What the police and lawyers tried to do to Charles was to entice him to sign a statement against his wife. They would not have needed Charles to lie if they had enough evidence of their own. Charles knew he legally did not have to testify against his wife. But he also knew that if they could falsify a warrant for his arrest, make his car look like it hit Dr. Sunshine, disregard an FBI forensic lab report, change a witness statement to put a female in the place of a male, remove photographs of the 1993 Lexus from the permanent file (this file was examined by me years later, and the photographs which were in the possession of Sgt. Collins were missing), have the arresting officer send an attorney to demand an incriminating statement from Charles, and have two attorneys suborn perjury, they could make his life a living hell. And that they did.

These police officers did not work independently; they had supervisors. Someone had to review their reports. How much did Sgt. Collins's supervisor, Sheriff Leon Lott, and Chief Stewart know? How could they not know what was going on?

In December 2001, Tshona's plea hearing was conducted. Many people gave testimonials about what a wonderful man Dr. Sunshine was to the community. His wife, son, daughter, and his father, who was in a wheelchair, were there. Even Sheriff Leon Lott spoke of his close relationship with Dr. Sunshine.

This plea was different. I saw officers who were involved in the investigation, knowing what they had done. I had seen their work. I had read the statements they had submitted and I was aware of some of the coercion and deception they used to get the warrant for Charles's and Tshona's arrest. The Sunshine family did not know the truth.

The prosecution presented their case. They presented the "shards of glass" that they said, "fit like a jigsaw puzzle" with glass missing from Charles's car. The evidence had already been dismissed by the report from the FBI as being not identifiable as glass from an automobile, but this did not keep the prosecution from presenting anything they could to imply that Charles's car was the car which struck Dr. Sunshine. Plus, they had access to both cars.

There was no mention of the black male passenger witnessed by Sharon Keels. I did not see Sharon Keels at the plea.

Solicitor Barney Giese and the authorities presented their questionable "evidence" knowing that it would not be challenged. The warrant was bad, probable cause was obtained from an untrained and unreliable person, evidence was destroyed, statements were changed, and the media ate it up. The worst part was seeing the Sunshine family and knowing that they did not know the truth. I did not know all the facts, but it hurt watching them believe what they were hearing. It was a carefully orchestrated event.

When it came time for Tshona to speak, Judge Manning read the charges against her. All she said was "guilty." Tshona never looked at the judge. She kept her head down. You could barely hear her voice. When asked if she had anything to say, Tshona said that the death of Dr. Sunshine was "by the hand of God." I was shocked to hear that. At the time, I thought it was an arrogant and insensitive remark. I would later find out that all the evidence led to the fact that Tshona had little or no involvement, and the fact that it was out of her hands meant that it was in God's hands.

Tshona pled guilty without revealing anything. There was no trial.

The family of Tshona Gaymon now became my adversary. They owed me over seven thousand dollars and refused to pay. They got what they wanted. Their attorney, Mr. Price, had recommended me to them. I later learned that one of the brothers of Forcina and Sandra worked for SLED, and he attended my first meeting with the family. So, I became an unwitting source for the prosecution. The Gaymon family never seemed interested in a trial or pursuing the problems with the evidence as Charles did. Mr. Price got the plea agreement and he was satisfied.

Tshona's family would not want the public to hear, in open court, Sgt. Collins's comment about them being "crack heads," Charles's statement about Forcina's drug problem, and Charles's introduction to Forcina's boyfriend, Johnny Brown, who was Sgt. Collins's initial suspect.

After Tshona's plea, Charles began having a problem receiving return calls from his attorney, Mr. Bolt. Mr. Bolt had done so well at the preliminary hearing. I assumed Charles did not owe any money to Mr. Bolt.

Shortly after Tshona took her plea, Charles told me he received a letter from Mr. Bolt advising him that it would be in Charles's best interest to take a plea to the charge of Failing to Report Certain Accidents, Accessory after the Fact, and Hit and Run. Charles was really angry. I could not believe it. I had no conversation with Mr. Bolt about it, and I was very disappointed. I had seen Dennis in the past go after the prosecution in a very deliberate and aggressive manner. That was not like him.

Over the next year and a half Charles would continue trying to get his charges dropped. The prosecutor would contact him from time to time through Mr. Bolt, and even without conferring with Mr. Bolt. Charles kept calling Mr. Bolt, and would even go by the office trying to get Mr. Bolt to convince the prosecutor to have his charges dropped so he could go on with his life. Sgt. Collins told Charles and me that they would drop the charges if Tshona went to jail. It was not enough that the charges were bogus, but they took his car, alleged that he was a criminal involved in the death of Dr. Sunshine, and his attorneys were all asking him to bow down and give in to the prosecutor. Charles had been through enough and was not going to back down to anyone. Charles always said, "Either drop the charges or give me a trial."

In the spring of 2002 Charles told me about a man named Fila Jameson. Fila was a twenty-nine-year-old black man who was a romantic friend of Tshona. Fila was a very close friend. From time to time, Charles and Tshona would separate; the relationship was stormy at times. Charles told me that Tshona would always want to be out "in the streets" and not taking care of Brandi. Laura confirmed the story that she would have to take care of the child while Tshona was out.

During one of the times that Charles and Tshona were separated Tshona became involved with Fila Jamison. Charles had moved back in with his mother, and Fila was sharing an apartment with Tshona in Columbia. The affair went on for months. Fila was with Tshona all the time. Fila got arrested on drug charges and Fila figured that Tshona had exposed him and broke off the relationship. In the meantime, Tshona was making up with Charles.

Fila was overwhelmed by Tshona. He did whatever she wanted him to do. Charles told me that she was the party girl and Fila was like a puppy around her. Charles had told me that Tshona was an attractive black female who could control men.

Soon after Charles and Tshona reconciled, Fila showed up at the apartment while Charles, Tshona, and Brandi were there. Fila was angry that Tshona set him up to be charged with a drug charge. He was also upset that Tshona had used him, both for the drugs and personally. Fila did not know that she was married to Charles, or that Charles even existed.

He came over to confront Tshona for "kicking him to the curb" and when he came and saw Charles, he went crazy. Fila had a gun. Fila fired off a few rounds into the apartment. No one was hit, but Fila was in big trouble.

Fila was represented by a public defender named Tara Lyons. I needed to talk with her client, so Charles and I agreed that I write Fila a letter through Ms. Lyons telling her that I had been retained by Charles on his criminal charges and that Charles needed information from Fila. Charles told me that he had no problem with Fila, and would not testify against Fila him. I sent the letter to the public defender on April 3, 2002.

During the next several months I was trying to get in touch with Fila. I needed to know about his association with Tshona and her friends and family. I even left messages with Fila's family.

I knew that considering the family history of Tshona, the admitted involvement of Forcina with John Brown, and the statement by Sgt. Collins that Tshona's family were a bunch of "crack heads," Fila would be a wealth of information. I also knew that the information he knew would lessen his sentence if he were convicted.

I called and made personal visits to the prosecutor's office. The chief investigator was the person I could talk to. That was Bill O'Neill. He was a good guy, and a company man. I knew that I could be straightforward with him. He knew I was working for Charles, and Bill also knew that I did not believe a damned thing that came out of the prosecutor's office with respect to the prosecution of Tshona and Charles.

I had handled many criminal defense cases, and had to challenge both the evidence and the use of evidence presented by the prosecution.

That was my job, to find flaws in the prosecution's case. That did not stroke the egos of many in the prosecutor's office. I had other clients who had experience with the prosecutor before Barney Giese was elected to that job. It was no surprise to them that I had another client to battle their office.

In 1994, I tried to get warrants for my clients against some gypsy palm reading swindlers. It took me five years to get warrants on behalf of my victimized clients, which annoyed the prosecution. Jim Stewart, who had been promoted to Captain Stewart, told me I would never get the warrants against the gypsies, who were a part of a worldwide organized criminal enterprise. This palm reader had never been arrested. (This was the same Captain

Stewart who took Sherma Doughty's statement.) I kept pushing because my clients were victimized. That took five years, but I got it. So, on the day of the settlement in which the gypsies paid out over thirty thousand dollars as part of the money they had scammed, the prosecutor told my clients not to pay me, stating that procuring a warrant for monetary reward was not ethical. That was just their jab at me, but my clients won.

After I sent the letter to Ms. Lyons concerning Fila, I was on the telephone with Bill O'Neill. Bill had a message to be delivered to me from the chief prosecutor, Barney Giese. Barney had never spoken a direct word to me. My first murder defense case was in January 1986, and I had been in the solicitor's office many times since then.

Barney told Bill to tell me "that Jim Simms must not be a very good detective. He followed me across town and I saw him behind me all the way." Bill was laughing his ass off. I knew what he was talking about so I had to shut him up long enough to tell him what Barney was talking about. Earlier that afternoon I was at a Starbucks coffee shop. Barney was there. Barney walked within a few feet of me and did not speak. He looked at me from a side glance, but I did not know if a greeting from me would be welcomed in a public place. So, I did not speak. When I gave that explanation to Bill, he told me that Barney told him that I had been following him across town, making turns in neighborhoods, and that Barney never travels the same route on successive days. I could not stop laughing. I told Bill to tell Barney that Barney had nothing to worry about. I had followed and caught hardened criminals, law enforcement officers, and FBI agents in acts of impropriety. I had no interest in where Barney was driving.

Bill had told me during our meeting that he wanted Fila convicted and needed Tshona and/or Charles to testify against Fila. Fila had shot up the apartment when Charles and Tshona were in the apartment. I told Bill that I already knew that Charles was not going to testify against Fila; he and Tshona had been having problems during that time and part of the problem was the fact that Tshona was being lured out "into the street" by her family. Charles said that Tshona had a family, a daughter, and that she did not need to be out there as she was. That was one of the major reasons for tension between them, according to Charles.

Charles had already had a run-in with the Richland County Sheriff's Department when he first came to Columbia from New York, the same sheriff's department that had made Charles's life hell and now needed him to testify against Fila. Charles told me he had operated a bar located on Leesburg Road outside the city limits of Columbia. This incident was related to me by Charles.

One night two deputies from the Richland County Sheriff Department came into the bar. They said they were there to be paid. Charles told me it was "protection money." They told Charles that if he wanted to stay open, he had to pay them. Charles told them to get out and had the bouncers show these cops to the door. A friend of mine had told me sometime later that he paid cash to two deputies who came into his business and the deputies told him the same thing they told Charles. My friend told me that the deputies did not know that they had been videoed as my friend counted out five thousand dollars on a glass countertop. A former drug dealer further told me that it was customary practice for some certain deputies to "shake you down," take your money and drugs, and then let you go. I recognized the names. I continued to hear the same thing over and over about a select few of these officers. I confided these incidents to persons I trusted. It was no secret.

Over the next months I tried to reach Fila through his attorney. I could not get a call returned very often, and always left a number for Fila to call me. I got a return call from Fila on September 24, 2002. I tried the number a number of times and got some of his relatives, but I was never able to speak to him on the telephone.

These guys really wanted Fila. Bill told me that he was going to subpoena Charles to appear and testify against Fila. I told Bill that giving Charles a subpoena would make no difference; Charles was not going to do any favors for the Solicitor's office since they trumped up a felony charge against him and allowed the first bogus charges to remain, if only as a threat and coercion. Bill was doing his job, but I told Bill in no uncertain terms that Charles did not owe that office a damned thing, and not to expect Charles to testify against Fila. I told Bill that they had these bullshit charges against Charles, jerked him around, and knew that people were trying to get him to lie for the prosecution. Bill said that if Charles was not going to testify for them that they would put him back in jail. I told Bill that Charles did not have to say a damned thing. I probably talked to Bill three or four times before Fila's trial date, and each time Bill would tell me, "You better make sure your boy is down here. If he knows what is good for him you will have him down here."

I told Bill that if he really wanted information about drug activity in the area, make a deal with Fila. Fila had been with Tshona for a while and he would know who Tshona was hanging out with. That would be was easy. They had Fila on a gun charge and Fila was looking at many years in prison. I also told that to Ms. Lyons, Fila's attorney. Fila was a wealth of information.

One of the calls I received from Bill O'Neill was on February 4, 2003. I told Bill that I was not Charles's lawyer and I was not making any legal suggestions to him. There was nothing else to investigate, and I told Bill that this story would make an informative book, and I told him I would be writing it. Bill told me that Charles trusted me. That was a compliment, and quite evident. Bill repeated the same thing; have Charles in to testify against Fila or they would revoke the bond and put Charles back in jail.

I talked to Charles about that call from O'Neill. Charles was not testifying. He was going to plead the Fifth. The prosecution was going to try to coerce Charles to do their work for them, again.

Charles was still trying to get an attorney to bring his case to trial. Charles had felony charges against him and not only could he not get Dennis Bolt to file the motion for the speedy trial, he was having problems getting return calls. He did not know the reason, but he would soon find out.

Charles told me the Solicitor's office kept calling his house. On May 6, 2003 Laura told me that the solicitor had called that day, and she answered the phone. Laura said, "They want Charles." They wanted to make sure he attended Fila's trial. They needed Charles and were not going to let him loose until they could use him up, regardless of the toll it would take on him.

Dennis Bolt was not returning Charles's calls, according to Charles and Laura. Charles sent Dennis a letter trying to get his file. Charles wanted a trial. He wanted to expose the real criminals in the criminal justice system. Charles told me he had talked to another attorney and that attorney was interested in taking the case.

I received a call from Bill O'Neill on Thursday, May 8, 2003. He wanted to meet with me. I told Bill that there was no more investigative work to be conducted on the matter but he still wanted to talk to me. My capacity was that of an author and a person trusted by Charles, not an investigator. Investigating Charles's case was over.

The following day I met with Mr. O'Neill in the office of the solicitor. Bill said, "It will all be over on Monday (May 12)." Bill still wanted Charles to take a plea. I reminded Bill that Charles was not testifying for the prosecution, and was not taking any plea.

On the day of Fila's trial, May 12, I showed up at the courthouse. Charles was there. Fila was with his lawyer and some of his family members. I got only a few moments to talk with Fila. Charles did not approach Fila, but Charles had no hard feelings against Fila. I explained that Charles was not interested in testifying against him, but Fila could help Charles. Fila told me he would get back to me, shook my hand with a ghetto handshake, and went into the courthouse with his family. The next thing I knew was that Fila had taken a plea and he was off to prison.

Charles did not testify against Fila. Charles told the prosecution that he was not going to testify against Fila. Charles did not help the prosecution at all. That might sound like a small matter, but it would be a large matter in the next months.

The prosecution did not talk to Fila about Tshona. Fila knew a lot. Bill told me they did not interview Fila.

Fila was off to prison. Charles was still being pressured to make a plea to false charges. The prosecution used Charles to coerce a plea from Tshona and Fila, but Charles never made any statement against either of them, and did not testify against them. They had used him up, but they still needed to save face.

Don't Get Arrested in South Carolina

Chapter Sixteen

The period after the December plea of Tshona continued to be a buffet of prosecutorial misdeeds. The Fila matter was just a blip on the radar.

Charles was still trying to get Dennis Bolt to return his telephone calls. In April 2002 Charles wrote Dennis two letters asking him to respond, and ultimately requesting permission to pick up his file. Eventually Charles got a letter from Dennis effectively suggesting to Charles that he throw himself on the mercy of the court.

Charles continued to make payments on the 1994 Lexus, which was still in the impound facility. The family needed that car for transportation. Charles was still making payments on the car but it was not available for him to drive. The SC Highway Patrol still had the car.

The daughter Charles raised was now in Georgia with a former lover of Tshona. The man claimed to be the father, and Charles and Laura had no money to contest it. Charles had raised Brandi from the time she was born. Brandi was nine years old when Dr. Sunshine was killed. A brief time before the death of Dr. Sunshine Tshona told Charles that Brandi was not his child.

Charles remembered an unidentified man coming to visit Tshona in the hospital when Brandi was born in New York but Charles did not think much about it. After Tshona was arrested, her family took the child and allowed the other man to take Brandi to Atlanta. Brandy called Charles "Daddy." Charles and Laura did not have the money to fight it—custody or paternity. No paternity test was done. Both Laura and Charles were devastated, and powerless.

Early in 2002 Charles called Sherma. I did not know he had called her, but that was no surprise. As he had done before, he would call people without my knowledge. He was a very smart man, but I really wanted to slow him down a bit. We had too many issues to address without going off on a tangent.

Sherma, who was supposed to have been in the car with Tshona, was no longer needed by the prosecution. Sherma told Charles, "The reason they did not bother me was because I was not in the car." She said she was never in the car. She also said that she knew the car that hit Dr. Sunshine was not Charles's car. She told Charles that the man that was in the car that killed Dr. Sunshine was a man named Carlos, who worked for Johnny Brown. Sherma also said that Carlos transacted drug deals from Hi-Line Imports. Sherma said that she was not going to be arrested because her father was an influential black man and he threatened to sue them if she were arrested.

Laura and Tshona used to work together at a department store named Dillard's. Laura told me that Carlos used to visit Tshona "while working at Dillards." They would disappear together and then return. Laura told Tshona that she knew what they were doing because Tshona's demeanor had changed. Laura also knew that Carlos was the chauffeur for John Brown; plus, K.C. Brown, John's brother, was a security guard at Dillard's. Laura told me that K. C. hung around her to try to make her uncomfortable. Laura was a lot stronger than any of those people thought.

Charles knew who Carlos was. Charles remembered that after the party at the Sheraton which Tshona attended, Charles found a photograph of Tshona and Carlos which was taken at a black strip club in Columbia. The club, Purple Passion, was located, oddly enough, next door to the Richland County Sheriff's Department. Charles had found the picture when it fell out of a telephone book. Charles tried to hide the picture in a closet. Charles got into an argument with Tshona about the picture, and Forcina, Tshona's mother from New York, was present during that argument. When Charles went back to get the picture the following day, it was gone.

I had to file a civil complaint against the Gaymon family because I never got paid the balance of the monies owed to me. My identity had changed from the great white hope to the "white devil," according to Sandra Lambright.

During the late afternoon of April 25, 2002, I made a stop at Charles's house. It was not unusual for me to stop by unannounced. I had no idea what I would hear would make me sick. Charles had received a telephone call from a female in prison. Tshona had been talking to her and identified two persons as the "kingpins" of a drug operation, and the connection was from Jamaica. Charles and I had openly discussed our personal knowledge of one of the local "kingpins"; the other person named was a high ranking local law enforcement official with whom I was all too familiar. Both men knew Charles and me, and different witnesses had told me about their cocaine use, forced sex, and an abortion paid for by the law enforcement official.

The next thing Charles told me was that the caller told him Tshona had a Jamaican visitor while she had been in prison. It was stated to Charles that Tshona had given a picture of Charles to the visitor. The reason for the visitor to have the photograph was to identify Charles and have Charles killed. I later was told this by two sources of my own. It got worse. Charles and I knew we had to get information from the prisoners, and two witnesses outside the prison, Sharon Keels and Sherma Doughty, would also be important.

On the following day, at approximately 3:00 p.m., I tracked down Sharon Keels. Ms. Keels was still employed with the postal service, but at that time she was assigned to the main post office located in downtown Columbia.

I asked one of the clerks for Ms. Keels. I waited for her in an area between the post office boxes and the outside glass wall. A large table was there for customers to use. As I waited next to one of the tables, a lady came to me and said she was told that I had asked for her. I asked if she were Ms. Keels. She said yes.

I told Ms. Keels my name, and that I had been retained by Charles Outlaw in the matter of the death of Dr. Harry Sunshine. I handed Ms. Keels my private investigator identification card, which was in a leather wallet. She looked at it for about fifteen seconds, and then handed my identification back to me.

I reminded her that in her statement she stated a black man was the passenger in the car she saw on Two Notch Road, and that she was right next to the car, having a close view of the "man." I also told her that Tshona Gaymon had taken a plea, had made no written statement of guilt to anyone, and claimed that it was "the hand of God" that killed Dr. Sunshine.

I told Ms. Keels that I had only two questions for her: Do you stand by your statement that a man was the passenger in the black Lexus? Did the authorities show you a line-up in order to identify the man you saw in the Lexus?

Ms. Keels asked to see my identification again. I handed it to her. She became very nervous. She handed the identification back to me. She turned to her right and said, "I need to talk to my attorney," and ran away from me down the lobby into an office. I stood there quite amazed but not shocked. Someone got to her, and she had to live with that. She never knew that being the good citizen and reporting what she saw would create a monster in her life.

That was a very scared woman. She was not talking. Why did she run? Why did she need an attorney to talk to me? Who was the attorney? She ran like I was chasing her. I never moved.

I went back to my office. I called Charles and told him that Sharon Keels ran from me. I also called Sherma to let her know what was happening. Sherma was always receptive to my calls. I asked her about the visitors that Tshona had in prison. Sherma told me that one of the persons visiting Tshona was Erica Brown, the daughter of Johnny Brown. Erica's nickname was Peaches. I had never heard that Johnny Brown had a daughter. Evidently Sherma thought so.

On April 30, I went straight to Charles's house. A bombshell would be dropped.

Charles showed me two letters. One of the letters was addressed to Tshona, and was from an inmate. Since Charles was the husband, he opened the letter. The inmate was referring to a time she and Tshona "hooked up" and "all the time I was diggin' you, you were diggin' someone else." She also made mention of her people on the street, with no names. The author of the letter had been arrested on drug charges in Florida and had been transferred to South Carolina.

The next letter was postmarked April 26, 2002 and was quite disturbing. The letter was from another inmate with access to Tshona. The letter was addressed to Charles. The letter said:

"Tshona is messing with some Jamaican guys. That's who did it. She gave me the name of 'Leon Lark.' She said them niggas is ready to kill and that's why Tshona won't say anything 'cause they will slice her up to [sic]. That's why she has hate in her heart for you calling the police but like (source name omitted) said she did that to herself and for her not setting you clear she just added more trouble on herself. She also stated, "one of them niggas is here and to watch our back 'cause she got you labeled as a snitch and she got a hit for you."

"She (Tshona) said these niggas know what you look like cause she got pictures."

"These niggas is out of Florida. They're Jamaican. One of them is here. And she gave me the name 'Leon Lark.' They have lots of money. (They) Can pay anyone off if they need to. These niggas have 'dreads' in their hair."

Dreads, like the man who took the car to Larry Aaron to be repaired?

Charles was on a hit list. Tshona was angry at him for calling the police, but she never told him why the police were looking for the car.

Charles got angry and called the police to bring it to an end. Little did he know that would turn his world upside down and almost kill him.

The person who wrote the letter had also called Charles on the telephone. She knew Charles's family and knew how to reach Tshona's family, and Charles. According to her source, Tshona had told some people in prison that "a black man was riding" in a different car and that Tshona was driving that car. It was "his" car, not Charles's car. The time was early on the morning of September 30, 2000. Tshona told her fellow inmates that she and the black man had been using cocaine in the car and the man wanted sex. Tshona told him that she needed to get home to Charles and she did not have time to have sex. The man got frisky and grabbed Tshona. Tshona slapped the man, and the man grabbed the steering wheel. When the man grabbed the wheel, the car ran off the road and hit Dr. Sunshine. They got out of the car, saw what they did, and left.

She also stated that the Jamaican that had visited Tshona had been given a picture of Charles, and Tshona wanted Charles dead. Tshona was angry at Charles for not letting her and her mother get away in Atlanta. Tshona also said

174

she never told Charles the truth about what happened that night and the identity of the black male in the vehicle.

As far as the person named "Leon Lark," I had a clever idea who that was, and we knew each other. That was not his real name, but it was close, close enough for me.

I thought the arresting agency, the SC Highway Patrol, would be interested in a death threat against my client. So, after leaving Charles's house, I went to the SC Highway Patrol office. I recognized one of the officers and explained why I was there. I had copies of the letters confirming the death threat. I was greeted by two patrolmen, and handed them the copies of the letters. One of the officers identified himself as the supervisor of Sgt. Collins but I did not write down his name. The two officers exchanged the letters after each read them. Both patrolmen told me they were well aware of the Sunshine case. After both read and exchanged the letters, they handed the letters back to me. I was told that there was nothing they would do about the death threat because Tshona had taken a plea and had been sentenced. I told them that did not surprise me since Sgt. Collins had arrested Charles and that Sgt. Collins would not be interested in Charles's welfare. Now the immediate supervisors of Sgt. Collins could not deny knowledge of the death threat. I had just told them. The officers told me to report it to Sheriff Leon Lott at the Richland County Sheriff's Department or the prison officials. I knew the sheriff's department would be just as excited in protecting Charles as the SC Highway Patrol, so I decided to go to the prison.

All I had was the first names of some inmates, approximate ages, and where they might be from. I researched the prison records and called the local police agencies to compare dates of birth to the ages I thought the witnesses might be. One was a local girl; the other grew up one hundred miles from here.

Don't Get Arrested in South Carolina

I went to the office of Elaine Pinson, the warden of the Women's Correctional Facility in Columbia. The prison was located on Broad River Road, and her office was in one of the prison facilities. I showed my identification to Ms. Pinson and showed her the death threat letters. Ms. Pinson advised me to contact an investigator within the prison system named Mr. Green. Ms. Pinson picked up the phone and got Mr. Green on the phone line. An appointment was made for me to see Mr. Green at 9 a.m. on the following day, May 1, 2002, at Mr. Green's office.

On the following morning, I was in the head office of the Department of Corrections, located on Broad River Road in Columbia. The office where I talked to Ms. Pinson was located at the rear of a different building. I met Mr. Green and we went up to his office. Mr. Green was a black male, probably in his fifties and wore glasses. I showed him my identification and gave him the copies of the two letters, one of which had the distinct information about the death threat. The names mentioned in the letters were a bit vague, so Mr. Green started looking at a computer screen and typing into the computer. He came up with the name of a person who we thought might be a person I might need to talk to. Mr. Green told me that he was not going to be able to accompany me to interview the women, and that I could talk to the women myself. That would not be unusual because I had interviewed many people in state and federal prisons and never had a problem or been turned away.

I left Mr. Green's office and went downstairs to the building Mr. Green directed me. The attendant at the gate needed authorization for me to enter the area. The attendant told me she would need to contact the general counsel for the department, which was in the same building as Mr. Green's office. The building was a short distance from the gate. I drove to that building and met with Barton J. Vincent, Deputy General Counsel for the Department of

Corrections. I explained to Mr. Vincent that I had been directed to Mr. Green by Ms. Pinson, and that I had met with Mr. Green that morning. I explained that Mr. Green authorized me to interview the source. Mr. Vincent gave me his business card and told me that if I had any problem to give the card to the gate keeper. The card read as follows: Barton J. Vincent, telephone 896–1278 (ext 8588), Deputy General Counsel, SC Department of Corrections.

I went back to the area where the source was housed. The black female was at the gate and she was very pleasant and helpful. She took my name and made the call to Mr. Vincent's office. After a few minutes, the lady at the gate made the request for the inmate to meet me. I was directed into a chapel, which was located a short distance to the right of the gate. I waited there at least fifteen minutes. It was cold in there. I had no idea what I was going to hear.

Chapter Seventeen

The chapel was small. There were religious paintings on the window. I figured that a corrections officer would accompany the source. After waiting in the chapel for at least fifteen minutes, a black female walked in alone. She told me her name and I did the same. I was hoping she would be the one I needed to talk to. She was.

The woman told me that she had been incarcerated at the Florida Women's Correctional Facility in Tallahassee, Florida until June 4, 2001 when she was transported to a facility in Columbia. A brief time before she left Florida she was in the dining facility in the women's prison and told me what she had heard in the dining room.

The source was working in the dining room. She overheard a group of loud women at a table. The table was occupied by a group of Jamaicans and they were rowdy. She heard part of the conversation and the words, "Columbia, South Carolina." The source went over to the table and told them that she was from Columbia and asked to know what they were talking about. They told her they were talking about the death of Dr. Harry Sunshine. The source did not know anything about that but she kept listening.

The Jamaican women told her that they were angry at someone named Supreme. A girl named Princess was married to Supreme. The Jamaicans said that a man had been killed in Columbia, and that Princess was involved. Princess had Supremes' car that night, but the cars were switched. Then something happened in Georgia. If Princess had been smart, she would have gotten away and not stayed in Georgia. Supreme was not involved in the death of the man. Supreme was somewhere else. The Jamaicans did not implicate Supreme in any of that, or any drug dealing.

Other Jamaicans had Tshona's apartment under surveillance. The women continued telling my witness that other Jamaicans cleaned out Princess's apartment before the police got to the house. They also took the black Acura that Tshona usually drove from the apartment. The Jamaicans were angry at Supreme for calling the police in Georgia, and said if Princess had left and gotten rid of the car, she would never have gotten arrested.

The Jamaican women then said that Princess was going to get Supreme for not letting her get away. Supreme had a price on his head.

The Jamaican women knew that the name of Tshona's daughter was Brandi. They said that Princess refused to give the child to Supreme. "They" were all angry at Supreme for calling the police on Princess.

I knew that Princess was Tshona; Supreme was Charles. The source referred me to another person who had been close to Tshona while she had been in prison. I had a nickname on a piece of paper, and an approximate age. Now I had to go do my work and identify that person.

I left the prison and called Charles. I met him and his younger brother in a restaurant. I told Charles what I had found out. Yes, they did put out a contract on him. Charles reacted as I expected. He was calm and not surprised. He said the people involved probably would want all of us dead. I agreed.

While I was going to do the research to identify another inmate housed with Tshona, I decided to identify one of Tshona's friends who I was told had been visiting her in prison.

The person visiting Tshona was named Peaches. Charles did not know anything about this person, other than the fact that he had heard that a person with that street name was visiting Tshona. I had not confirmed the visits, but Peaches needed to be identified.

It was learned that Peaches was Erica Brown. Erica and Tshona attended A.C. Flora High School together in Columbia. My research revealed that Erica had an address in Atlanta, and that there was an address connection between Erica and a relative of Johnny Brown.

Mr. Brown was the president of the security company called Ampro. Ampro went bankrupt after a few years, backed by the former governor of South Carolina, John West. During the time that Tshona was in jail, I was told that Mr. Brown had left Columbia, and moved to Atlanta.

Why would Peaches be visiting Tshona in prison? She stated that her relationship to Tshona was "friend" and then "cousin" at different times on the sign-in sheet. It had been stated by Forcina to Laura Outlaw that Forcina had an ongoing romantic relationship with Johnny Brown. As was stated before, Charles was introduced to Johnny Brown in the presence of Tshona and Forcina in Summerton, South Carolina. If Peaches was a "cousin" then who were the fathers of Tshona and Peaches?

Early on May 8 I talked to Charles. I probably talked with Charles every day. He told me he finally talked to Dennis Bolt. Dennis told Charles that the prosecution could hold the case as long as he wanted to, and he (Dennis) could not make the prosecutor try the case. We begged to differ, but it made no difference. Dennis said he would meet with Johnny Gasser, the prosecutor, next week.

Not being the attorney, I had to rely upon the intellect of other sources to help Charles. I had a close friend who was an attorney in the northeastern U.S. She told me that the case involving Charles could be addressed as a violation of the 1983 Civil Rights Act, in which the police and prosecutors could not use excessive force, unreasonable methods, or racial profiling, and that the actions taken by the authorities would "shock the conscience" of the public. The fact that Charles was not given a preliminary hearing for nine months could be part of the grievance.

A day or so after I interviewed the first source in the prison I went back to the building where Ms. Pinson's office was located and I asked for Ms. Pinson. The lady at the window told me that Ms. Pinson was not in. I told the lady that I was here to interview an inmate.

The prison activity was defined by the old saying, "While the cat's away, the mice will play." The guards and inmates looked like they were having a party. The noise level was unbearable. Rap music was being played in the office located to my left. The guards and the women inmates were laughing and "yucking it up" so loudly that I could hardly hear myself think. The person who said he was in charge was a big fat black man named Mincey. Mincey told me that I was not going to talk to anyone, and that he was in charge. It was not worth my time to try to carry on a conversation with Mincey. So, I left.

I went to the headquarters of the SC Department of Corrections to speak with Mr. Vincent. He was not in. I left a message for him to call me.

My notes revealed that calls were made to Ms. Pinson and Mr. Vincent on May 10 at 9:20 a.m. That was very important based upon the events that were to follow. The return message I received from Mr. Vincent was that I would need to make a formal request to see any other inmates.

On May 13, I submitted a fax to Mr. Vincent requesting to interview an inmate. The fax stated that I was not in the employ of any attorney, just my client. I also reminded him that I had interviewed many persons in prisons, and referred him to Captain Joseph Dorton, who headed the SLED Regulatory Division. The division handled licenses for private investigators. I had nothing to hide.

Later in the day I tried to reach Mr. Vincent, but he could not be reached. That afternoon I went to Vincent's office. People in the human resources area said he was not in. I then traveled a short distance to SLED headquarters. I talked to Lt. Profit, and showed him a copy of the death threat and the request to interview an inmate, which was faxed to Mr. Vincent. I went back to the SC Department of Corrections and went to the human resources office. Ms. Thrailkill stated I probably should talk to a man named Richard Stroker. I went back to my office and called the number for Richard Stroker. His office was closed, and the time was 4:30 p.m.

I knew something was wrong. Someone got to someone. I smelled the rat. I had no idea what was going on or the identity of all involved, but I kept SLED informed of what I was doing.

On the following day, May 14, 2002, I called Mr. Vincent at 8:24 a.m. Mr. Vincent told me that the warden had denied me access to the prison. I immediately called SLED and reported that I had been denied access to the prison. No agent was available but I was told someone would call me back. If I had done something wrong I was damned sure I was not going to involve the agency which issued my license. Why would I open myself to scrutiny if I had done something improper?

I then talked to Richard Stroker, who had been referred to me by Ms. Thrailkill in human resources. He told me he was going to contact Warden Pinson.

I made a call to Dennis Bolt's office. Dennis was still representing Charles. I told Dennis's paralegal, Tannie, that I needed to get to interview the second source. Dennis did not help.

It looked like I was going to be stonewalled. I did a thorough search of the names of the persons in the prison, and the locales they were from. Based upon information I had, I determined the exact name of the person I needed to see. I figured she was going to be in prison for a while, as her release date was more than a year away.

SLED Agent Craig Perry called me on May 15, 2002 at 10 a.m. I told him about the problem getting into the prison. He told me he would be looking into it.

Agent Perry called me back at 3:40 p.m. on the afternoon of May 23. His attitude had changed and he was very defensive. Agent Perry told me that I had been accused of deceiving the people at the prison. Mr. Green denied giving me the authority to talk to a prisoner. Perry told me he would call me when he returned from his assignment.

I was mad, frustrated, confused, puzzled, but not surprised. I told Perry that I would not have involved a regulating agency having authority over my license and expose any misdeed if I had done anything improper.

I decided to write a letter to the inmate I could not visit. I put in a note for her to call me and/or add me to her visitors' list. A few weeks later I got a call from a lady named Andrea Moseley. She told me that the person I needed to talk to had received my letter, but she wanted me to deal with Ms. Pinson. I had no problem with that, but I did not know that there had been a big miscommunication between Ms. Pinson and me, in addition to the fact that Mr. Green lied about authorizing me to interview the first source. I got my letter back, returned to me from the inmate.

In the meantime, Charles was getting no active participation from Mr. Bolt. Mr. Bolt had been telling Charles to take a plea and let the case go away. If Dennis had not realized it by then, Charles was going to fight this to the end.

My friends and professional contacts thought I was a bit crazy to continue with the case. I had seen too much to stop. The lies to the judge to get a warrant, the attempt at coercion by police, attorneys and a former judge, the corruption, and for what? The lies and cover-up had now affected me. Now someone was lying about me. Something was wrong in the prison. That had never happened to me before. I would not know the full extent of the lies until a year later.

On May 23, 2002, I mailed a letter to Mr. Vincent. I explained the entire scenario with respect to my visiting the prison, as well as my visits with Ms. Pinson, Mr. Green, Mr. Vincent himself, and my source. Mr. Vincent was made aware that a copy of the threat was left with Captain Dorton, as was mandated by my professional license. I basically told Mr. Vincent that his ambivalence with respect to my client having a death threat emanating from his facility was unfair to my client, and if someone threatened a member of his family, he certainly would not ignore it. A copy of the letter was sent to Captain Dorton and the Chief of SLED, Robert Stewart.

I heard nothing from Mr. Vincent, Captain Joseph Dorton, or Chief Stewart. SLED was under scrutiny for the curious lab results which post-dated the FBI reports and contradicted the FBI reports, as well as statements taken from witnesses. SLED would not be interested in me interviewing another potentially damaging witness.

It would be close to a year before I would know the truth about the false allegations made against me at the prison. I knew that information concerning the real car and Tshona's involvement would come out in court, but there was no trial date set for Charles and we had enough to expose the authorities. That was the reason I did not push for the explanation.

SLED Agent Perry told me that I misrepresented myself to someone at the prison. I had never done that before and never needed to do that. Agent Perry also told me in January 2003 that I told one of the prison officials that I was with law enforcement, and that Perry could have me arrested for that. If it had been true, he would have arrested me on the spot. He was approaching me in an accusatory manner, and he said he had "evidence" that I had not seen, but he did not present any evidence to me. I knew that he was a pawn in a larger scheme, and Agent Perry was just being told what to do.

On March 5, 2003, I called SLED to see what "evidence" Captain Dorton had in my file at SLED. As of April 10, 2003, I had not received any response from SLED, so I wrote another letter to Captain Dorton. On April 23, 2003, I received a package from Lt. Mike Brown of the Public Information Office at SLED, and wrote Captain Dorton to respond on May 28, 2003.

The package included four items regarding statements made by officials at the prison. Parts of the statements are listed below, with comments after the statement highlights.

May 20, 2002 Interview of Pat Thrailkill, Assistant Director of Human Resources.

Details:

- Ms. Thrailkill met with Mr. Simms, who was upset because he could not see inmates at the women's facility or see Bart Vincent.
- Ms. Thrailkill asked Simms for I.D. and was presented with private investigator identification.
- Ms. Thrailkill contacted Mr. Vincent's secretary, who stated Simms needed an appointment to see Mr. Vincent.

- Ms. Thrailkill ended meeting informing Mr. Simms to make an appointment prior to coming to see Mr. Vincent.
- End of interview.

Comments (J.B. Simms)

These facts were not in dispute. I had no need to misrepresent my credentials. I did not need an appointment to see Mr. Vincent on the first visit.

May 22, 2002 Interview of James Green, Investigator, Department of Corrections.

Details:

- Mr. Green met P.I. Simms on or about May 1, 2002. This was an unscheduled meeting and Simms wanted permission to speak with inmates.
- Mr. Green informed Simms only the Warden of an institution could give that approval.
- Mr. Green stated Simms had information relating to violence which in some way was associated with inmates.
- Mr. Green stated Simms wasn't concerned w/reporting information to corrections or law enforcement, just interviewing inmates.
- Mr. Green informed Simms if Richland County was involved with his vital information, they would have access to inmates.
- Mr. Green stated when Simms departed he states he is going to the Woman's Center and Mr. Green contacted Ms. Pinson.

End of interview report.

Comment (J.B. Simms) Addressing Specific Assertions Made by Mr. Green.:

The meeting with Mr. Green was not unscheduled. During my visit with Warden Pinson, she called Green while I was sitting across from her at her desk. She was aware that I was to meet with Mr. Green, an investigator, on the following day at 9:00 a.m. She made the appointment.

I did not remember if Mr. Green stated that only the Warden could authorize a visit to an inmate, but Ms. Pinson referred me to Green, and Green told me to go interview the inmate alone because he was too busy to accompany me.

It was true that I had information relating to violence; I had the death threat letter.

I told Mr. Green I would tell him if I had any information which would identify the source of the threat. Mr. Green should have had access to the visitor log of Tshona Gaymon to see who had been visiting her, but I assume that did not occur to him.

If Mr. Green contacted Warden Pinson after I left our meeting, with Green knowing that I was en route to interview a specific inmate, known to both of us and identified by Mr. Green, and if Ms. Pinson did not authorize me to interview the inmate, then why was the interview allowed to take place? Mr. Green and Mr. Vincent knew exactly where I was going, and no one stopped me.

I gave Mr. Vincent the same information and he did not protest my visit. There would be no reason to prohibit me from talking to any inmate unless the inmate protested.

Mr. Green lied to the SLED Agent Perry. SLED Agent Perry did not see the contradictions that were evident in my comments section of Mr. Green's interview.

J.B. Simms

Affidavit of Barton J. Vincent, July 16, 2002, selected paragraphs.

- On May 1, 2002, I was contacted by Operations at Women's Correctional Institution about Investigator Jim Simms requesting to visit an inmate at that institution. I requested information as to whether Investigator Simms was working for a law firm or whether he was associated with a member of the South Carolina Bar.
- While Operations was getting this information, Investigator Simms drove from Women's Correctional Institution to the Headquarters Building for the Department of Corrections.
- I received a call from Human Resources that Mr. Simms wanted to speak with me. I walked down to the Human Resources Office and spoke with Mr. Simms.
- During this discussion, Mr. Sim [sic] represented to me that Warden Pinson had approved him to visit Inmate (deleted), but that someone else at the Institution was preventing him from visiting.
- Based on his representation that he had approval from the Warden, I verified with Operations at Women's Correctional Institution that Mr. Simms should be allowed to visit.
- I later discussed this with Warden Pinson and she indicated to me that Mr. Simms did not have approval from her to visit anyone at Women's Correctional Institution.
- On May 13, 2002, I received a voice mail from Investigator Simms indicating that he wanted to visit another inmate. I returned the call and left a message for Mr. Simms that he needed to put

any request in writing. I later received a fax from Mr. Simms, requesting permission to interview another inmate at the Women's Correctional Institution.

- Having discussed Mr. Simms's prior requests with Warden Pinson, it came to my attention that Warden Pinson had not approved any other prior visits by Mr. Simms. This was contrary to his representation to me on May 1, 2002.
- Warden Pinson also told me about a phone call of May 9, 2002 during the re-naming ceremony at Women's Correctional Institution. She indicated to me that she was told that her husband was calling her during the ceremony. Because she thought it was an emergency, she took the call, only to find out that it was Mr. Jim Simms.
- Because of his acts of dishonesty, I did not immediately take any action on Mr. Simms's faxed request.
- On the afternoon of May 13, 2002, I was contacted by the Department's Human Resource Office. They told me that Mr. Simms was in the Office, requesting that I see him. Because he came without an appointment and I was preparing for Court, I declined to see him at that time. I indicated that Mr. Simms needed to make an appointment.
- Mr. Simms became agitated that he could not see me and requested to see the Assistant Director of Human Resources. After the Assistant Director saw Mr. Simms, she requested that our security personnel escort Mr. Simms from the building.
- Overall, Mr. Simms has provided false information to me and other employees of the Department and has acted in an unprofessional

manner. At this time, he is not allowed to visit any of our institutions, nor is he allowed in the Headquarters Building.

Signed, Barton J. Vincent, Deputy General Counsel

J.B. Simms Addressing specific assertions made by Mr. Vincent:

- I told Mr. Vincent, as I told Ms. Pinson and Mr. Green, that my client had received a death threat. I had evidence of the threat. All parties saw the letter. I, as a private investigator, having been retained by a defendant, wanted to know if we could find out what the prospective assailant looked like, and who it might be. This was made perfectly clear to all three parties. Whether I was retained by a law firm or associated with a member of the SC Bar was not an issue. This was murder for hire, and my client was being targeted.
- When Mr. Vincent knew I was downstairs, he walked down to talk with me. I had no appointment. There was no appointment necessary. Mr. Vincent developed the "appointment" defense in order not to discuss the matter.
- I told Mr. Vincent that I had met with Mr. Green, and that Mr. Green assisted in identifying the inmate who needed to be interviewed. I also told Mr. Vincent that Warden Pinson had directed me to Mr. Green. Mr. Green then told me to interview the person myself because he was too busy to accompany me.

- Warden Pinson directed me to Mr. Green. If Mr. Green had thought I needed permission from Ms. Pinson after meeting with him, then he would have directed me to Ms. Pinson or called her himself. Mr. Green did not call Warden Pinson while I was there.
- Evidently Ms. Pinson was stating that no visits were approved. During the first visit I had with Warden Pinson, she never indicated that I would not be approved to visit an inmate. She was the one who called Mr. Green and referred me to him. Warden Pinson knew from the beginning that the only reason I came out to the prison was to interview the inmate. I knew that if the inmate were to be interviewed by a member of SLED, the Richland County Sheriff's Department, or the SC Highway Patrol, they would have no interest in preserving the life of Charles Outlaw. It was up to me to do it.
- During the initial meeting with Warden Pinson, she directed me to Mr. Green and gave no indication that I would not be able to interview any inmates. I certainly advised Warden Pinson of my experience in these matters, having interviewed literally hundreds of inmates and defendants. She was well aware I wanted to interview an inmate. Ms. Pinson would have no reason for the denial of my request.
- In reference to the telephone call she received from me on May 9, 2002, I did recall making the call. My notes reflect a different date, but the date in my notes could have been an error. I certainly did not use the name "Pinson" to identify myself. As I wrote to Captain Joseph Dorton of the Regulatory Division at SLED, the noise level in the prison was so bad at the

reception area, plus the fact that, when asked who was calling my response would be "Jim Simms," the person answering the telephone very possibly would have mistaken that for "Pinson." Having the male voice, plus the fact that the employee answering the telephone would have a different language orientation and education level than I did, it was very likely that was what happened. I had no reason to hide my identity. I wanted them to know who I was, and who my client was.

- There were no acts of dishonesty on my part.
- The first time I came to the headquarters building Mr. Vincent stopped his "work" and came downstairs to talk with me. The indication for me to make the appointment was made through his secretary and not Mr. Vincent personally. Mr. Vincent did not speak to me on that occasion.
- There was no reference to security personnel in the building in the interview/statement given by the Assistant Director of Human Resources, Ms. Thrailkill, to the SLED agent. If that did happen, it would have been noted.
- There was never any false information given to any of the prison employees, nor to the office of the General Counsel. The refusal of the visit by office of the General Counsel, plus the fact that SLED did not furnish copies of interviews for a year, compounded the problem.

Affidavit of Elaine K. Pinson, July 16, 2002, selected paragraphs.

- That I first had contact with Private Investigator Jim Simms on April 30, 2002. On this date, he came to Women's Correctional Institution (now called the Graham Correctional Institution) to interview Inmate (name deleted) for his client, Charles Outlaw. Mr. Simms indicated to me that Inmate Tshona Gaymon might have solicited someone to kill his client.

- Because this matter involved possible criminal behavior, I contacted the Department's Division of Internal Affairs. On May I, 2002, Mr. Simms met with Investigator Green.

- I received a call from Investigator Green on May 1, 2002 indicating that Investigator Simms was coming to my institution and wanted to visit Inmate (name deleted, she was the source). I did not allow the visit.

- After speaking with Investigator Green, I called our Office of General Counsel and was told to have Investigator Hair with the Department to interview Inmate (name deleted). I was also instructed to have the investigator contact the Richland County Solicitor's Office and Sheriff's Department so that they could investigate any criminal activity. I informed Investigator Hair. Investigator Hair replied that her supervisor is Investigator Green and she would need to speak with him.

- At no time did I approve a visit for Investigator Jim Simms to interview any inmates at Graham Institution or any other institution.

- I had a second conversation with Investigator Simms on May 9, 2002. On this date, the Department was having the renaming ceremony at this institution.

- While I was hosting the ceremony, I was told that "I was needed up front. That my husband was calling." This concerned me because my husband usually does not call me at work, and he knew about the ceremony. Thinking that it must be an emergency, I took the phone call. To my surprise, the caller identified himself as Investigator Jim Simms. I was very upset that I was told my husband was calling, only to find out it was Simms.

End of statement of Elaine Pinson.

J.B. Simms: Addressing specific assertions made by Warden Pinson.

- Ms. Pinson admits contacting Mr. Green, and knowledge of the May 1 meeting, which was scheduled from Ms. Pinson's office.
- I was not aware of any call made from Mr. Green to Warden Pinson after the meeting with Mr. Green. I advised Mr. Green, and it was agreed, that if I determined a verifiable threat to my client, I would advise him of the same.
- I had no knowledge of the involvement of Investigator Hair. Mr. Green certainly had the option of having Investigator Hair accompany me during the interview. The fact was that no one at the prison had the background information I had, and an interview conducted solely by prison officials would not be a complete and thorough interview. Also, the Richland County Sheriff's Department and the Richland County Solicitor's Office had no interest in the well-being of my client, who they knew had information which would attack the integrity of both offices.
- At no time during our initial conversation of April 30, 2002, did Warden Pinson intimate, indicate, or imply that I would not be

interviewing an inmate. She called Mr. Green and she made the appointment.

- The call I made to the prison to speak with Warden Pinson, and the final sentence of her statement answered all questions. "I was very upset that I was told my husband was calling, only to find out it was Simms." The important words in the statement were the words "I was told my husband was calling." Warden Pinson was "told" it was Simms. When I would identify myself on the telephone, I would never say "Private Investigator Jim Simms" or "Investigator Simms" or "Investigator Jim Simms." I always identified myself as "Jim Simms." The person who took the call was a black female who had such a strong Southern black dialect that I had to struggle to understand what she was saying, and evidently, she did not understand me either. If she heard "Pinson" rather than "Jim Simms" and conveyed that to Warden Pinson, that was a mistake on the part of the prison employee, not an act of unethical behavior on my part.
- End of statement.

There would be no ethical reason why I would not have been able to interview the inmate. The authorities knew why I was there. Tshona was a very high-profile prisoner, a celebrity among the inmates.

I did not get the chance to respond directly to the persons involved until I got these documents almost a year after the incident. I sent a letter to Captain Joseph W. Dorton at SLED on May 28, 2003 outlining some of the above contradictions in the statements and the confusion surrounding the fact that a person in the prison "thought" Warden Pinson's husband was on the phone.

That was only one of the issues going on at the time. Charles was still trying to get Dennis Bolt to demand a trial. The issue of the prison debacle would be used to our advantage; it would be the fact that they did not want me to interview the inmate who would be able to identify the person Tshona asked to kill her husband.

I was not the story here, but I smelled a rat and I pushed the envelope for my client and for the truth. SLED Agent Perry's reaction to the allegations made by prison officials, plus the fact that I was not given the opportunity to debate or clarify the statements, was very suspicious behavior. SLED was part of the prosecution, and they seized upon the opportunity to attempt to attack my credibility and taint my testimony. The prosecution knew that the credibility of SLED, the SC Highway Patrol, the Richland County Solicitor's office, the Richland County Sheriff's Department, and a former Chief Justice of the SC Supreme Court would be compromised by a competent and brave lawyer. No attorney in South Carolina was willing to do that, but we were willing to "put the skunk on the table."

Don't Get Arrested in South Carolina

Chapter Eighteen

I sent a letter addressed to both Captain Dorton and Chief Stewart, both at SLED, requesting a meeting on the subject. They did not respond. They knew that I knew the truth, and what they were hiding.

I found out from Charles that he had been talking to other attorneys, and that did not surprise me. Charles was an angry young man. No one was listening to him. All the information I was furnishing him was thought to be for naught because his attorney would not demand the trial he deserved.

Charles had continued to make payments on the 1994 Lexus, as well paid for insurance and taxes for the vehicle. He thought the case could not have any more twists, and that he would not be victimized by the police anymore. He was very wrong.

During the time that the 1994 Lexus was impounded by the SC Highway Patrol, Charles continued to make the payments to his insurance company to insure the vehicle. My notes revealed an incoming call on March 29, 2002 from a man named Rob Ramos, and a telephone number for Sierra Claims Company. That was during the same time that I was trying to reach Fila Jamison and his attorney, Tara Lyons.

On April 25 at 2:15 p.m., I made a call back to Rob Ramos. Mr. Ramos told me that a claim had been made against Charles's car and he needed to know if the insurance was still in effect. It was a weird question, and I did not know the answer. The South Carolina Highway Patrol still had the car. Ramos told me he did talk to Dennis Bolt but that Dennis was very short with him. Charles then called and told me that he did talk with Mr. Ramos.

A brief time later Charles received a letter stating that Sierra Claims Company was to pay a death claim against Charles's insurance policy on the 1994 Lexus. The policy was to pay fifteen thousand dollars to the family of Dr. Sunshine. How was the insurance company going to verify the claim that Charles's car was the car that killed Dr. Sunshine? That information had to come from the Solicitor's office and the SC Highway Patrol. Charles questioned the payment of the claim.

On May 23, 2002, the same day SLED Agent Perry accused me of deceiving the officials at the prison, Charles telephoned Rob Ramos to discuss the death claim being paid to the Sunshine family. Ramos, who was the adjustor, told Charles that he was told by someone in the Solicitor's office that Charles had no charges pending, and did not detail who he spoke with. No charges pending? There had been no trial which proved that Charles's car hit Dr. Sunshine, but someone in the Richland County Solicitor's Office had been talking to Ramos. Ramos told Charles that he did not remember who he talked to in the Solicitor's office, but I am sure that the conversation was noted in the file and the name of the person was also written in Ramos's notes. Was the Sunshine family made to be an unwilling partner to insurance fraud?

After Charles confirmed that the claim had been paid, he called Sierra Claims office again. He was told that Rob Ramos no longer worked there. Ramos could not be reached.

A few days after July 19, 2002 Charles received a letter from First Citizens Bank, the bank that financed the 1994 Lexus. Charles did not know that the letter was coming; Laura got the letter while Charles was actually at a branch of First Citizens Bank making a payment on the car. The branch bank was located directly across the street from the location of Hi-Line Imports on North Main Street. It was the same location I had entered and recovered the second bill of sale issued by Suhail in order to sell Charles the car. The letter was from a person named Todd Branham in the collection department of First Citizens Bank.

Laura called Charles on his cell phone as Charles was in the bank making the payment. Laura told Charles that she had the letter addressed to him from the bank and she opened the letter to read it to Charles.

Dear Sir or Madam:

On July 19, 2002 First Citizens Bank and Trust Company of South Carolina recovered the 1994 Lexus which served as collateral on the installment loan we made to you on September 27, 2000. This is to notify you that after July 29, 2002, these goods will be sold at Public Sale to the highest bidder.

This sale will be conducted in accordance with the security agreement and the SC Uniform Commercial Code. If you desire, you may redeem these goods before the sale by paying off the full sum of $5,393.77, plus any expenses and fees allowed by law. After the sale proceeds have been applied against what you owe, you will receive any surplus. However, if the proceeds of the sale are less than the amount owed, you may be held responsible for any deficiency as allowed by law. A copy of the sale showing the date of sale, the time, and the location where the sale will take place is enclosed. If you have any questions, please contact us.

Sincerely, Todd Branham

How did the bank get the car? The car was at the impound facility of the SC Highway Patrol. The car was evidence in the case against Charles, but the car was also evidence in his case against the SC Highway Patrol, SLED, and the Richland County Sheriffs' Department. The car had now been compromised. The authorities knew that; they sabotaged the case Charles had against them. Who was going to be accountable for this?

The two charges against Charles, Failing to Report the Accident (having property damage in excess of $1,000.00) and the indicted charge of Accessory after the Fact, were still pending. How could the prosecution attempt to get a verdict or even a trial if they could not use the car as evidence? Sgt. Collins told Judge Davis there would be no trial. The trial Charles wanted would not be him presenting a defense; Charles was ready to attack the prosecution and put them on the defensive. We had the bullets; we just needed a gun.

Charles was furious. The Solicitor's office would not have allowed the car to be released from the impound area if they were going to use the car as evidence. Charles had been making the payments on the car and First Citizens Bank had no legal right to be in possession of the car or send that letter. There must have been communication between First Citizens Bank, SC Highway Patrol, and Mr. Giese at the Solicitor's Office. This was a concerted effort to deny Charles access to his car and to compromise the chain of evidence so Charles could not have the 1994 Lexus independently examined. The car should have been released to Charles, but First Citizens Bank and the authorities kept Charles in the dark.

Charles told me he had never been late on a payment. Even Laura told me that she had to make some of the payments. Again, I had to take Charles's word. Charles had told me many things during the past year or so. He never lied to me.

Charles went "Charles" in the bank. He became very intense, but not rude. He knew that was just a continuation of punishment by the authorities. He told the teller about the call from Laura. The teller brought up Charles's account on the computer and the account was not delinquent. Charles called the collection department and gave them an earful. Laura then got a call from the bank. A man at First Citizens Bank told her to come get the car. He told her that the police brought the car to the bank and told the bank official to tell Charles that his car had been repossessed. Todd Branham did as he was told, but it was hard to imagine that Todd Branham, who was a regular collector with no authority to repossess a vehicle without approval, would do that and sign his name on the letter, but he did. No one had been in trouble for anything that they did to Charles regardless of who they were.

Laura told Charles to meet her at First Citizens Bank. There was a parking lot near the bank building. Laura, Charles, and Charles's brother met and went to the gated parking area. Laura showed a letter to a guard and they were allowed entry. A bank official met them and repeated that the authorities brought the car to the bank and told them to repossess it. Laura told me that the bank official even helped boost the battery. The reclamation of Charles's car was videoed by Laura and Charles. Charles never knew how long it had been parked there. The bank had a big problem. They would have more problems later.

What was the bank doing with Charles's car? Who in the bank was discussing this matter with Barney Giese at the prosecutor's office? Who gave Mr. Giese the authority to release evidence to a third party and not the owner of the property? Dennis Bolt did not challenge Mr. Giese concerning the compromising of the evidence.

Some months later, Charles paid off the loan on the car. Now he wanted the clear title. Charles still had a repossession on his credit bureau report. Why?

Somehow the bank was so intimidated by the authorities, or in concert with them, that the bank compromised their own policies and consumer laws, and entered a repossession on Charles's credit bureau report. What a case Charles had against the bank.

When you finance a car, the title of the car is kept by the bank, in the file. A form would be filled out by the bank and the purchaser of the car. This form and the title would be sent to the highway department, and the form would indicate that the bank had a lien of a certain amount on the vehicle. The new title, showing the lien by the bank, would be returned to the bank. The person financing the vehicle could not sell the vehicle because the bank had the title, and the lien was printed on the front of the title. When the loan was paid, a bank officer would sign his name in the designated space on the back of the title, which showed that the loan was paid, and the owner was free to sell the car if he wished.

I had worked at lending institutions and specifically at First Citizens Bank some twenty years earlier. I oversaw all installment loans collections for the city of Columbia, which included loans made by anyone authorized to make a loan whether it was a branch manager or any lender at the central office. Any delinquent loan came across my desk, and was my responsibility. That was before the bank was automated by computer. We had the files. We had the securing documents. We had car titles which had liens recorded. There was no reason to remove a title from a file. No reason at all. I assume the authorities were not aware of my experience in banking.

While Charles was trying to get his title, he told me that Todd Branham, the collection employee, stated that a SC Highway Patrol officer came into the bank and asked for the title to Charles's 1994 Lexus, which was in the loan file. Mr. Branham did not remember when this happened, but that information would be in the file. The officer took the title.

Why would a SC Highway Patrolman come to the bank and take the title of a car? When did he do this? The bank employee did not like to have to answer Charles's questions, but Charles was not letting him off the hook. The bank employee offered Charles a check for the price of a duplicate title, thirty-five dollars. There was no more information to come from that employee.

Charles had no intention of cashing the check from the bank. He still would not have full possession of his car. He could have asked for a duplicate title from the SC Department of Transportation, but the lending institution had the lien and Charles would still not be able to sell the car or get a loan on the car.

Charles made more phone calls to the bank. During one of the later calls Charles was told by a different person at First Citizens Bank that the bank had lost the title. That was no surprise. At first Charles was told that the title was handed over to a SC Highway Patrol officer. The bank changed their story and said they lost the title. The bank was in bed with the prosecution and was doing what the prosecution could not do, which was eliminate Charles's car and compromise the chain of custody so Charles would not have access to the car for inspection. Charles was arrested two months after the loan was made. The file must have been pulled and put in a special place. No one loses a title. The employee who Charles first talked to was too scared to lie. The next employee tried to tell Charles that the bank lost the title.

Charles kept the car. He was hoping he could use the car to exonerate himself, noting that the vehicle still did not have the damages consistent with having killed Dr. Sunshine. The headlight was intact, the fender was not crushed, the door post was straight, and the hood was not damaged. The prosecutor did not want to try this case, and I told that to Bill O'Neill every chance I had. Barney Giese would not risk us exposing all we knew, or he knew, but we did not know how he would keep it from happening.

Charles checked his credit again. The repossession was still on his credit report. The female bank employee at the branch on Main Street had told Charles that no repossession showed up on his loan. Todd Branham had sent the letter on July 19, 2002, telling Charles that the bank had the car. Charles continued to call First Citizens Bank. I had done contract investigative work for that bank and was familiar with some of the people in that collection area. I told the persons I knew personally that they had a big problem. Charles called many times to get an answer. He was being ignored.

In the second week of May 2003, ten months after telling Charles that the bank had repossessed his car, Charles received the following letter from First Citizens Bank:

May 8, 2003

First Citizens Bank 1230 Main Street Post Office Box 29 Columbia, SC 29292

RE: Charles Outlaw Loan #: 114059676

The above referenced loan was reported as a repossession in error. A letter has been forwarded to the credit bureaus to reflect the correction. The correction should show no repossession, past due pay history and the balance paid in full.

Sincerely, Ronnie Jordan Vice President

Retail Credit Support Manager

Charles received no letter from the bank with any explanation of how they got his car. Who from the bank discussed the illegal transfer from the custody of the SC Highway Patrol and Barney Giese? Mr. Giese had possession of the vehicle since November 2000. Charles got no apology from the bank for "erroneously" reporting a repossession to his credit report. Who told First Citizens Bank to do that? Who at First Citizens Bank took the risk of knowingly filling false information on a credit report? It was an attempt to discredit and harass Charles, and it worked. It was like Todd Rutherford said, if Charles was not on the team of the prosecution, his life would be miserable. Charles was like a mouse in a box, being poked with a sharp pencil through the top of the box. He could not see who was poking him, but he knew he could not relax, because if he was not looking up, he was going to be poked again. What a way to live. He lived under constant stress. Charles did not know the agenda of the authorities. All Charles knew was that he was going to get poked again.

First Citizens Bank: Repossession Letter

FIRST CITIZENS BANK OF SC
1314 PARK STREET
P.O. BOX 29
COLUMBIA, SC 29202

July 19, 2002

CHARLES M OUTLAW

Re: 114059676

Dear Sir or Madam:

On July 19, 2002 First Citizens Bank and Trust Company of South Carolina recovered the 1994 Lexus which served as collateral on the installment loan we made to you on September 27, 2000. This is to notify you that after July 29, 2002 these goods will be sold at Public Sale to the highest bidder.

This sale will be conducted in accordance with the security agreement and the SC uniform Commercial Code. If you desire, you may redeem these goods before the sale by paying off the full sum of $5,393.77 plus any expenses and fees allowed by law.

After the sale proceeds have been applied against what you owe, you will receive any surplus. However, if the proceeds of the sale are less than the amount owed, you may be held responsible for any deficiency as allowed by law. A copy of the sale showing the date of sale, the time, and the location where the sale will take place is enclosed. If you have any questions, please contact us.

Sincerely,

Todd Branham

First Citizen Bank: Notice of Sale of Charles' auto (evidence)

FIRST CITIZENS BANK OF SC
1314 PARK STREET
P.O. BOX 29
COLUMBIA, SC 29202

Notice of Sale

Take notice that First Citizens Bank and Trust of South Carolina will sell to the highest bidder for cash at Public Auction at 906 Washington Street, Columbia, SC 29201 at 9:00 AM on the day of July 30, 2002; the following described property:

Vehicle: 1994 Lexus

Serial #: JT8JS47E8R0078755

This property is being sold as a result of noncompliance of the terms and provisions of a note and security agreement given by CHARLES M OUTLAW to First Citizens Bank, dated, September 27, 2000, and covering the aforesaid property.

First Citizens Bank: Retraction of Repossession of auto/evidence

First Citizens Bank

1230 MAIN STREET
POST OFFICE BOX 29
COLUMBIA, SC 29201

May 8, 2003

RE: Charles Outlaw
Loan #: 114059676

The above referenced loan was reported as a repossession in error. A letter has been forwarded to the credit bureaus to reflect the correction. The correction should show no repossession, past due pay history and the balance paid in full.

Sincerely,

Ronnie Jordan
Vice President
Retail Credit Support Manager

Chapter Nineteen

Charles called me on the morning of August 15, 2003, almost three years after the death of Dr. Sunshine. The prosecutors still had not brought Charles's case to trial. The prosecutor had released the evidence to a third party, thus contaminating the evidence Charles could use against the police and prosecution. Now Charles was going to tell me something else which he did not reveal to me at the time it happened.

Charles was a proud man, and he did not want to have to call me to help him at every turn. As I said before, he was forever talking to professional people, television stations, newspapers, and attorneys, trying to draw some attention to the matter.

On that morning Charles told me he had received a letter, dated August 3, 2003, from Johnny Gasser, the Assistant Solicitor (Prosecutor) for Richland County. The letter, directed to Charles, told him he had to be in court for roll call.

Charles went to the Richland County Courthouse the following week as directed by Mr. Gasser. There must have been hundreds of persons there for the roll call that day. Charles stayed in the courtroom waiting for his name to be called. All persons with pending cases had to appear at the roll call. After they appeared, they were given another date to appear at a next roll call. That would happen a couple of times. In the meantime, the prosecutor's office and the attorney for the defendant would work out some deal and then the defendant could enter a plea, usually to a lesser charge unless the defendant was blatantly guilty and had no way out.

Charles sat in the courtroom all day. He had to be attentive because the names were not being called in alphabetical order. Even though the officers in the courtroom kept order, the milling around and dull roar of attorneys and defendants talking made it difficult for Charles to hear what Ms. Levy, the prosecutor's office manager, was saying from the bench while she called the name of each defendant.

The number of defendants was so many that Charles had to come back after lunch. After lunch, Charles returned to the courtroom for the afternoon session and never heard his name called. He got worried because his name had not been called, and if the judge thought Charles had not answered, or had not appeared, a bench warrant would have been issued for Charles's arrest.

After all the names had been called, Charles went down to the front of the courtroom. He told the clerk that he had a letter stating that he was supposed to be in court that day but he did not hear his name called. To his amazement, he was told that his name was not on the list to appear.

Charles became worried. He went to the Solicitor's office. He was not supposed to be in there, even in the waiting room. There was a sign that no defendants were to be in that office. Charles needed answers. He saw Investigator Bill O'Neill. Charles told Mr. O'Neill that his name was not called and that Charles did not know what to do. Mr. O'Neill said that he would check it out and left the waiting area.

O'Neill returned and told Charles that Johnny Gasser wanted to talk with Charles. The attorney representing Charles, Dennis Bolt, had not been seen in the courtroom, and if Charles's name had been called Mr. Bolt would have to go before the judge with Charles. But now since Mr. Bolt had not been seen, how could Mr. Gasser talk with a defendant without an attorney being present?

Charles had not been receiving return calls from Mr. Bolt. The last letter he received from Mr. Bolt suggested that Charles enter a plea to the charges and fall upon the mercy of the court. So much for Charles's defense team. Dennis did what none of the others did; he got Charles a preliminary hearing. After that, Charles became expendable.

While waiting for Mr. O'Neill to return, Charles clutched his file. Charles went nowhere without his file. The file was comprised of copies of documents plus items I had generated for Charles's defense. Mr. O'Neill led Charles into the office of the solicitor. Charles noted that Mr. Bolt was not there, and Charles told Mr. Gasser and Mr. O'Neill that he might be retaining another attorney who quoted a fifteen-thousand-dollar retainer. Charles had in his possession transcripts of two telephone conversations, one that I had with Todd Rutherford, and one that Laura had with Rutherford. Both conversations were recorded before Charles picked up his file from Mr. Rutherford. Charles handed copies of the transcripts to Mr. Gasser and Mr. O'Neill.

After reading the transcripts, Mr. Gasser told Charles that he would reduce the charges against Charles to some simple charge if Charles would take a plea. Charles refused any plea. He told them he wanted a trial and walked out.

When Charles told me about the meeting with Gasser and O'Neill, he also told me about the letter that Gasser had sent him requesting his presence at the roll call. I told Charles to look closely at the letter.

As Charles examined the letter he had received from Mr. Gasser, I told him to look under Mr. Gasser's signature. Charles told me that there was no typing under the name of Mr. Gasser to indicate who actual typed the letter received by Charles; there were no initials under the signature of Mr. Gasser, which indicated that Mr. Gasser could have typed the letter himself. I told him that he should call Mr. Gasser's secretary to see if she typed the letter. Charles told me he called the secretary, mentioned her by a name I was familiar with, and told me she denied writing the letter.

All we knew was that Charles was invited to a private meeting with the prosecutor. At the time Charles did not know if Mr. Bolt had relieved himself of representing Charles. If Charles had no attorney, we assumed that Mr. Gasser could legally talk with Charles. Rutherford told me that Charles would be in big danger without an attorney.

I felt that Charles was in a position of power, and had stood fast in the face of being accused of being an accessory to the death of Dr. Sunshine. After being jerked around for three years, Charles still had no answers about the events which led to the death of Dr. Sunshine.

On Wednesday, September 10, 2003, I received a telephone call from Bill O'Neill. Bill said, "Simms, we're going to drop the charges against Charles. They're doing it today. The clerk's office will have the paperwork." My heart fell out. I was numb, and I was drained.

I called Charles immediately. Laura took the call. She was over-whelmed. She then gave the phone to Charles. I told him the news, but I was to find out later that the solicitor was going to have a parting shot.

Unknown to me, Charles had been talking with another attorney. This attorney, Eleanor Dean, a black female, had told Charles that she had worked in the Solicitor's office and could help him. Charles told me that he had given Ms. Dean a thousand dollars to help him. Charles later learned that Dennis Bolt had sent Mr. Gasser a letter requesting to be relieved as counsel. Mr. Gasser had taken a job with the U.S. Attorney's Office, so I did not know who was prosecuting the case. The attorney, Eleanor Dean, told Charles that she knew everyone in that office and she would find out what was going on and help him.

So, Charles trusted another attorney to do something for him. When I called Charles to tell him that Bill O'Neill had called me, Charles was happy, but then he told me about the black female attorney, to whom he gave money to help him. Charles knew that the attorney had no input on the charges being dropped because Bill O'Neill did not call her, he called me.

Remember the statement made by Todd Rutherford, who was Charles's first lawyer (if you discount Jerry Finney)? Todd told me that if the Solicitor's office catches Charles out with no lawyer, they will make life a living hell for him. Well, Charles held his ground, and Rutherford misjudged Charles. But what did Rutherford care? He had five thousand dollars of Charles's money and did not actively defend Charles because he did not want to offend his former boss, Johnny Gasser. The SC Supreme Court dismissed a formal complaint Charles made to the Disciplinary Committee against Rutherford. Charles filed the complaint to Henry Richardson, the head of the Disciplinary Committee. He told Mr. Richardson that Rutherford took the money, failed to allow Charles to have a preliminary hearing on six separate occasions, and did no discovery. Mr. Rutherford had been elected to the SC House of Representatives from an urban area of Columbia. Plus, he had friends in the prosecutor's office. Todd Rutherford was neither disciplined nor sanctioned by the committee.

Charles also made a complaint against the Finneys, Jerry and his father, the former Chief Justice of the SC Supreme Court, Ernest Finney. Charles outlined the behavior of Finney coming to the jail at the request of the arresting officer, and the suborning of perjury. That complaint was denied by Mr. Richardson just like the one against Rutherford.

Don't Get Arrested in South Carolina

All these complaints had to be made. Charles needed to document everything and have all our witnesses listed. I used the word "our" because the prosecution would attempt to discredit me as a witness for the defense. I was ready. I had access to witnesses they did not know (the test drivers of the car in September 2000), plus the fact that I had compiled volumes of paperwork contradicting many of the statements taken by the SLED agents. Collins knew I knew about the 1993 Lexus and I could not wait to see that evidence come out, but those pictures Collins showed Charles and me would disappear. But, I had been ready, and kept reminding Bill O'Neill.

Charles called the office of Ms. Dean. She told him that she did not know about the charges being dropped. Charles figured out that if she had known, the prosecutor would have called her instead of calling me. The fact was that Charles was still under the impression that Dennis Bolt was his attorney; he did not know Dennis had withdrawn. That did not stop Ms. Dean from taking money from Charles. Charles was pretty mad at her. He left his house on Wednesday September 10 and went straight to the office of Eleanor Dean. He went to ask her what she had done to help him. Ms. Dean told Charles that she had made some telephone calls and spoken briefly with the new assistant solicitor, Mr. Pascoe. Charles and I found out later, independently, that she did call the Solicitor, but never talked to anyone.

On the morning of Friday, September 12, I called Bill O'Neill again to see if the charges had in fact been dismissed. He said yes. I asked specifically about both charges, the Failure to Report Certain Accidents (misdemeanor) and Accessory after the Fact (Felony). Bill told me that one was dismissed on Wednesday the tenth; the other was dismissed on this day, September 12. The conversation was, "OK, Simms, the charges have been dropped. It is over. Go get a fucking life." That did not offend me; it was pretty funny. Bill was okay. I knew where he was coming from, and he and the Solicitor's office knew that I would protect and stand up for my client if he were being wronged.

At noon, I had lunch with Eric Ward, a writer for a tabloid paper in Columbia called the Free Times. The paper printed articles that the daily newspaper The State would not print, such as indiscretions by a former governor, having been surprised having a "Bill Clinton" moment with an assistant. I thought this would be a story Eric would run with.

He took lots of notes. He wanted to see the car and talk with Charles and Laura. I told him I would arrange it. I also told him I was compiling all my information to write a book on the matter, so the "hat" I wore had been an investigator and/or an author.

Eric did not call me back. I called him a week or so later. He did not want the story.

I contacted a writer at The State newspaper. The writer told me that his bosses told him they would not print the story unless Charles sued the SC Highway Patrol and the State of South Carolina. No one would print the story.

After I had lunch with Eric Ward I went to the Richland County Clerk of Court office. I asked the clerk in the Criminal Section for Charles's file. I pulled out some papers. I saw the original warrant and the following:

- The Commitment, dated December 1, 2000, stating that Charles had been charged with Failure to Report Certain Accidents, Warrant Number G638281. The arresting office was listed as T.B. Collins. The bond was set at $250,000.00 (The original bond, $250,000.00, was for an unclassified misdemeanor.)

- The second Commitment, dated December 2, 2000, stating that Charles had been charged with Failure to Report Certain Accidents, Warrant Number G638281. The arresting office was listed as T.B. Collins. The bond was set at $25,000.00, stating "Bond Reduced by Judge Womble 12/01/00 PM." (That was after Sgt. Collins called Laura Outlaw and told her that "he" had the bond reduced as a favor to her and Charles.)
- Indictment, dated August 17, 2001, stating that the Grand Jury for the Court of General Sessions had handed down a "True Bill" on the charge of ACCESSORY AFTER THE FACT, stating, "That Charles Outlaw did in Richland County between September 30, 2000 thru November 29, 2000, knowing of the commission and completion of the felony, Reckless Homicide (56-5-2910) and/or Leaving Scene of Personal Injury Accident Death (56-5- 1210(A)(3), by the principal felon, Tshona Gaymon, aid, harbor, and assist such felon to escape detection or arrest or otherwise avoid he consequences of the crime." On the opposite side in an area labeled VERDICT, the following words were found, "Nolle Pros w/leave to restore. (symbol for defendant) aided in several investigations" and the signature in combination print and cursive writing "Pascoe/A.M." The witness was listed as Sgt. Tom Collins- SCHP. The SC Code was listed as 16-1-55 & 17-25-30, CDR Code 2415 & 0788, Class: Fel/F & UNC.

This much we knew; Sgt. Collins was the only witness to testify to the Grand Jury. We never saw a transcript of that hearing. We never knew what he told the Grand Jury.

The notation "Nolle Pros" means no prosecution. Someone signed Pascoe's name, and initialed it with "A.M." We were not told who A.M. was, but I did know someone with those initials.

"With leave to restore" means they could bring the charges back again if they damned well felt like it. My reaction was "be my guest."

The most outrageous part of the documentation, which was not only on the indictment, was the statement "Defendant aided in several investigations." I hope Pascoe and "A.M." were told to write this, having trusted the person telling them to write it, or being commanded to do so. This was a lie. They tried to make Charles into a snitch. Charles was not a snitch. To state that Charles "aided in several investigations" meant that Charles assisted the police to solve a crime or convict a criminal. That never happened. Charles never testified against Fila. Tshona took a plea. Charles fought the prosecutor for almost three years and refused to take a plea. He would not take a plea. He would not give a statement against Tshona like Sgt. Collins, Jerry Finney, Judge Finney, and Todd Rutherford tried to get him to do, or take a plea as Dennis suggested. So, Charles was not a snitch; he was the enemy of the prosecution. They tried to make it look like they had pressured Charles to help them. It was a lie but it would never go to trial. Sgt. Collins said that from the beginning.

Basically, Sgt. Collins testified before the Grand Jury to punish Charles for having the Preliminary Hearing. Rutherford was right about that; he stated that if the Preliminary Hearing was held, the prosecutor "would trump up some bullshit charges against Charles." Then the prosecution tried to make Charles appear to be a snitch.

- Screening Sheet, dated September 10, 2003. Defendant: Charles Outlaw. Warrant Number: G638281 Charge: HIT AND RUN ASOL (Assistant Solicitor) 82 Disposition: A check mark in   a square box. The initials NP (Nolle Pros) lined out and the letters "DISM" (dismissed?) Explain: w/l to restore. Defendant aided in several investigations."

Hit and Run? The prosecutor wrote Hit and Run on Charles's Screening Sheet, using the same warrant number they used for the initial improper charge of Failing to Report Certain Accidents. So, the war- rant number used for the unclassified misdemeanor was now a warrant number for the felony of Hit and Run? Again, they wanted people to think that the reason the charges were dropped was because Charles helped the prosecution. If you think that might have happened, then you never have not read this book.

Pascoe's name was on the screening sheet, with the initials A.M. next to his name, and those charges were dropped on the Wednesday Bill called me.

- Screening Sheet, dated September 12, 2003. Charge: Accessory after the Fact. The box labeled "NP" was "x-ed out" and the letters "WLTR (with leave to restore) written in the explanation area.

Pascoe's name was on that sheet too, but the initials P.G. were next to Mr. Pascoe's name.

I left the courthouse with the dismissal sheets, and could not de- scribe how I felt. In a way, I wanted to see Bill, but I knew I would have probably made some comment I could not repeat so I just kept my eyes straight ahead. There was no real feeling of victory. The hours I had spent on this case as a private investigator and collecting the facts to write this book were long and hard. I could not compare the attacks on me professionally to what Charles and his mother Laura went through, but this was not easy. Had I been tilting at windmills? Maybe. Did I get paid for a tenth of my work? No. Charles was now out of work. No one would hire him. Sgt. Collins and the prosecution would see to that by publicly demeaning him. Laura was on a fixed income. I must have needed to exorcise a demon in me to make me keep going. It damned sure was not for the money.

I called Laura before I left the courthouse and I knew she would be waiting. I remember it was hot outside, but I was sweating anyway. I drove past the University of South Carolina football stadium; I could stand it no longer. My eyes were filling up. I thought if I did not wipe them that the tears would not come out. I was wrong. I figured if people saw me wiping my eyes while I was driving they would think my dog had died. I pulled off the road for a minute before I got to Laura's house.

She did not need to see me like this. We won that part of the battle, but we paid quite a price.

I gave Laura a couple of copies of the Screening Sheets. It was a good thing her door was closed because if her neighbors saw her hugging a white man, tongues would wag. Of course, Laura was happy. We won this part. Now Charles knew that he had to get an attorney to file the lawsuit against Sgt. Collins and the State of South Carolina.

Dismissal Sheet: Accessory After the Fact

DISCHARGE FROM JAIL ☐

SCREENING SHEET

1. Prepare this case for Grand Jury: _____
2. Name of Defendant: Charles Outlaw
3. DP or Warrant Number: DP01404
4. Charge: Accesory After the Fact
5. Officer/Agency: _____
6. Please Subpoena: _____

O GS 40 06313   Reviewed by: _____
OR   Date: _____
Pending Unindicted
                ASOL # _____

* *

DISPOSITION

☐ Dism. ☒ AF ☐ Remanded ☐ Dismissed at Prelim ☐ Failure to Appear ☐ PTI ☐ Restore ☐ Judicial Dismissal ☐ Other

Explain: W/ LTR _____
_____
_____

OR

Date of Failure to Appear: _____
Date Bench Warrant Issued: _____

                Solicitor: Yasoee/Rg
                Date: 9/12/03

Dismissal Sheet: Hit and Run (falsely charged)

DISCHARGE FROM JAIL

SCREENING SHEET

1. Prepare this case for Grand Jury: _____
2. Name of Defendant: Charles Outlaw
3. DP or Warrant Number: G638281
4. Charge: Hit & Run.
5. Officer/Agency: _____
6. Please Subpoena: _____

____ GS 40 ____
OR ____
Pending Unindicted   ASOL # 82

Reviewed by: _____
Date: _____

* *

DISPOSITION

☐ ☑ ☐ ☐ ☐ ☐ ☐ ☐
Dism. NP Remanded Dismissed Failure PTI Restore Judicial Other
DISu   at Prelim to Appear   Dismissal

Explain: W/C to restore A aided
in several investigations

_____

OR

Date of Failure to Appear: _____
Date Bench Warrant Issued: _____

Solicitor: Pascoe /Am
Date: 9-10-03

Chapter Twenty

There was no mention in the media of the charges against Charles being dropped in September 2003; no newspaper article, no television, no radio. There was no satisfaction for Charles and, of course, no apology from anyone. No one would know about the lies that the prosecution wrote, stating that Charles helped with other cases.

Two months later Charles was in the hospital. He had a heart attack. Charles had been a very healthy male in his early thirties. He did not drink much, and he did not smoke. Laura called me to tell me. I went to the hospital on a Sunday morning in late November. Charles was hooked up with tubes, hoses, and monitors. I told him he could not die because he had not gone after the persons who did this to him. Months later Charles had to have a heart transplant. Stress kills, just as effectively as a hit man.

Charles knew he had a claim against Sgt. Collins and others. Charles wanted people to know what happened to him, and he did not want it to happen to anyone else. Charles was both curious and interested in what was really in the files of the agencies involved in the case. I told him that he needed to file a Freedom of Information Request to each of the agencies. I told him I could file the request as any private citizen could.

The Freedom of Information Request is submitted to a public agency; it mandates that the agency make available to you the information in that particular file. If you ask for information about a case that is ongoing, you will not get to the file until the case is over. That was why we waited to get to the file. If Charles had been given a trial, we would have had access to the file by subpoena. But, since they decided after almost three years that they did not want a trial, they dropped the charges and figured that we would go away. Not a chance.

Anyone can file a Freedom of Information Request. A private citizen can send a letter citing the Freedom of Information Act and the agency must respond. You do not need any special credentials. You do not need to be an investigator, work for a newspaper, or be involved with an attorney. Charles could have done it himself but the stuff would have to be reviewed by both of us, so I told him I would do it. He knew I was compiling the information for a book.

On February 10, 2004, I mailed a Freedom of Information Request to the following agencies:

- Richland County Solicitor's Office
- Richland County Sheriff's Department
- South Carolina Law Enforcement Division
- South Carolina Highway Patrol

In short, all these agencies were supposed to reply by making the files available for inspection and/or copying everything in the file and giving it to me. What was surprising was that each agency handled each inquiry in a unique way. The manner in which they responded, and the material in the files, plus the material that was not in the files, spoke volumes with respect to their intent on not letting Charles, me, or the public, know the truth.

In the body of the Freedom of Information Request, I asked for the entire file involving the death of Dr. Sunshine. I noted seven items in the request, stating that the request was for the entire file including but not limited to the following items:

- Records of all black Lexuses inspected and photographed by any law enforcement agency and in your possession. The results of all forensic examinations of all black Lexuses, including both from Hi-Line Imports, were specifically requested.

(I knew that the photographs of the 1993 Lexus, taken by Sgt. Collins, would prove the existence of the car. All the agencies were aware that I knew about it.)

- Copies of all statements made by any witness, including Sharon Keels, the postal worker who gave a statement to authorities approximately October 31, 2000, in which she stated that the passenger in the vehicle was a black male. The statement by Suhail Najjar should also be included. Results of any line-up queries given to Ms. Keels, used to identify the occupants of the vehicle she observed were also requested.

(We knew that Sharon Keels could not identify Tshona as the passenger in the vehicle.)

- The Report of Examination submitted by FBI analyst Maureen Bradley, which included the statement, "Based upon the examination of these items of evidence, no OEM automotive paint is present."

(We knew that the FBI report dated October 31, 2000 predated the lab reports from SLED dated January 24 and 25, 2001. FBI Agent Espie was the liaison, and criticized the SLED report.)

- Records of all direct communication, either by telephone or in person, with any representative of your office and Charles Outlaw.

(We knew that the Solicitor sent Charles a letter telling him he needed to appear in court in August 2003. His name was not even on the docket.)

- All charges made against Charles Outlaw subsequent to the preliminary hearing.

(The charge of Accessory after the Fact was made after the preliminary hearing. Sgt. Collins testified to the Grand Jury.)

- All communication between your office and the other agencies involved in this case.
- A list of all attorneys who contacted your office on behalf of Charles Outlaw, and any written correspondence received or sent.

I told Charles that I sent the letters. The responses differed one from another. The following are the responses:

Richland County Sheriff's Department, Sheriff Leon Lott

Sheriff Leon Lott did not respond, as mandated by law. Sheriff Leon Lott was very much involved with the case. Sheriff Lott spoke at the sentencing of Tshona Gaymon. I was told that Sheriff Lott was also familiar with the initial suspect, Johnny Brown, who was the boyfriend of Tshona's mother, Forcina.

Since I had heard nothing from Sheriff Lott, I went to the Record Division on February 18, 2004. The lady there was very nice. Her name was Sharon Moody. Ms. Moody told me that no file was available for me to review. Ms. Moody further stated that she had talked to Capt. Jim Stewart, who was the first officer to interview Sherma Doughty. Capt. Stewart told Ms. Moody that all the files on this case were sent to the South Carolina Highway

Department and that the Richland County Sheriff's Department had no records on Dr. Sunshine's death in their office; not even an incident report was available. I asked Ms. Moody to contact Capt. Stewart to request that he put into writing that Sheriff Leon Lott had no record available of the death of Dr. Sunshine.

On March 3, 2004, I called to speak Capt. Stewart and spoke with Ms. Moody again. She was very nice and told me she would talk to Capt. Stewart again to get a letter from him or Sheriff Lott denying having any records on the case. No response was received.

Richland County Solicitor's Office, Solicitor Barney Giese

Mr. Giese did not respond to the FOI until I called a secretary named Babs on March 3, 2004. Mr. Giese was mandated to respond long before this, but he ignored the FOI request just as Sheriff Leon Lott had done. He was the chief prosecutor, but ignored the law.

Soon after I made the call, I received a letter from Mr. Giese. I assumed Mr. Giese was in a hurry or not focused because it was evident that the letter was typed by him personally, and the letter was not dated. Mr. Giese "answered or addressed" the seven items I listed, which were to be "included but not limited to" these seven items. So, Mr. Giese repeated the seven items and responded to each one.

Basically Mr. Giese stated that his office was not a repository of any records for any law enforcement agency. The FBI report should be obtained from the FBI. Records of arrest warrants were available through the Richland County Clerk of Court's Office. He refused to disclose any record of any communication with any other agency in this case. He also refused to disclose any communication between his office and any attorneys stating to represent Charles.

Where was the copy of the letter that Mr. Gasser wrote Charles? Where was the bond form from the bonding company, ABC Bonding, which had Jerry Finney's name on it? The Solicitor's office had no file on the death of Dr. Sunshine, just like Sheriff Leon Lott.

South Carolina Law Enforcement Division

I received a letter from Lt. Mike Brown advising me that he had received the request. He and the SC Highway Patrol were the only ones to respond.

I called Lt. Brown on March 3, 2004. Lt. Brown told me that he did not have the file with him. Tad Reed had the file and that Agent Reed was "working on the file." "Reed is pulling out information from the file." I reminded Lt. Brown that Reed was the investigating officer for SLED, and that I wanted all the information. Lt. Brown was not offended by my statement. I had known him since about 1986 when he was working in the Regulatory Division inspecting private investigator offices. He told me that they had to redact information. He told me that the file had to be inspected and redacted, blacking out some names and social security numbers. The fact was that I had seen what should have been in their file during the investigation. What was "not" in the file was as important.

The photos taken by Jimmy Winders were found. The photos showed the horizontal scrape on a fender, a cracked fog light, a headlight intact, door post not damaged, hood not damaged.

Photo line-up sheets were in the package. Information about Charles' car was there. The SLED forensics result was in the package.

What was missing was important:

The FBI report from October 31, 2000 was not in the file.

That was interesting because when Chip Price sent me a copy of the discovery material he had obtained from the Solicitor's office; the FBI report was in the file. Of course, this information did not link Charles' car with the damage to the bicycle, nor could the FBI identify the glass that SLED stated was automotive glass.

There was no information about the 1993 Lexus which had been on the lot at Hi-Line Imports at the time the authorities, including SLED, went there on October 20, 2000. They conveniently omitted that information.

I knew that the original warrant was signed by Judge Michael Davis, who was a magistrate on the opposite side of the county from Charles' apartment. On March 1, 2004, I went to talk to Judge Davis.

I told Judge Davis that the information on the warrant was not correct; Sgt. Collins stated on the warrant that he, the Affiant, had seen the damaged car, Charles' car. Collins also attested to the fact that Charles' car had a tag number. I told the judge that the car never had a tag, and that the car was recovered having a paper tag.

Judge Davis told me that he had talked to Sgt. Collins about the death of Dr. Sunshine a number of times before asking for a warrant for Charles' arrest. Judge Davis specifically stated to me that he knew that Johnny Brown had been the original suspect. He stated he thought it was Sgt. Collins who alleged the involvement of Johnny Brown. I explained the connection between Johnny Brown and the mother of Tshona Gaymon, and the fact that it had been stated that Tshona had been receiving a visitor in jail named Peaches, who was said to be related to Johnny Brown. Judge Davis told me he knew Peaches, whose real name is Erica, and Judge Davis also thought she was related to Johnny Brown.

Charles was right. He was right all along. He had been hearing that Brown was the original suspect but there was no information in any material from the discovery to the Solicitor or to Sheriff Leon Lott with the name Johnny Brown indicated.

Johnny Brown had connections to these people from his former law enforcement position to running Ampro, the security company originally backed by the former governor of South Carolina, John West.

I had a reason to be at SLED headquarters during that time. I told Captain Dorton what I had been told by Judge Davis. The response from Captain Dorton was, "We do not owe Johnny Brown any favors."

The speculation that Johnny Brown was the original suspect was not speculation much longer.

South Carolina Highway Patrol

The contact person for the Department of Transportation was Sheridan Spoon. Mr. Spoon was a young attorney, and a pleasant man to deal with. I made an appointment to meet with him on March 5, 2004. He told me that Sgt. Collins had the file and he needed to get the file from him. That was not comforting.

Mr. Spoon had a huge box of information. Some of the information was on ringed binders. Some was in large envelopes. Nothing in the file had been redacted, but there was one glaring omission from the file; the photographs of the 1993 Lexus were missing. Where did Sgt. Collins put the photos of the Lexus, or to whom did he give the photos?

He shrugged his shoulders, sighed, we both kind of smiled, and he pushed the boxes of information toward me. This poor guy had to sit and watch me go through two big boxes of material for at least an hour and a half. He did get up to go to the bathroom and get something to drink. I kind of felt sorry for him. Someone sent this poor guy down here to deal with this mess.

I took notes on significant material in the file. These would be items I would need to copy to show Charles. I gave the list to Mr. Spoon. Months later I called him and told him that I had not heard from his office. Mr. Spoon told me that he had called me and had no response. I did not remember him calling or I certainly would have gone to get the information. He set up another meeting and I went through the material again. I gave him the list and he got the copies made. I picked them up sometime later.

The following is a list of some of the material found in the file:

- The letter from Johnny Gasser to Charles dated August 3, 2003 asking him to appear in court.
- A yellow sticky-note with the writing "atty Finney."
- Database inquiries on Sandra Lambright (Tshona's aunt) and Mamchu S. Jeff (Tshona's cousin).
- An audio-taped conversation of James Brown, dated October 19, 2000. James Brown was the witness who saw Charles and Tshona on the morning after the accident. It was interesting that the interview with James Brown predated the statement given by Sharon Keels. How did the police know to talk to James Brown before Sharon Keels put a black Lexus in the picture?
- An "updated statement" from K. W. Reed (SLED agent) to Sgt. Collins dated November 21, 2000.

- A search warrant dated November 28, 2000 for Charles' apartment. Sgt. Collins filled out the inventory sheet.
- An auto inventory of Lexus automobiles at Hi-Line Imports. The inventory revealed that the 1993 Lexus that Charles and I had identified, black in color, having the last numbers of the vehicle identification number being 35717, had been obtained by Hi-Line Imports on June 21, 2000. There was no record of it having been sold.

(Charles was right again. We had evidence that the police knew the 1993 Lexus was on the car lot. But guess what was not in the file? The pictures of the same car, the wrecked 1993 Lexus, the same ones we saw in Sgt. Collins' office in May 2001, were missing.)

(Someone removed the photos from the file. They were not there. If Charles and I had not seen them, no one would have never known they existed, except for the two law enforcement officers who were with Sgt. Collins when he took the photographs. But we saw them. Collins knew it. I told Bill O'Neill I saw them. They would not keep that information to themselves. The case was blown before it got started. Sheridan Spoon had told me that he got the box containing the records from Sgt. Collins.)

- A subpoena for telephone records for Laura's home telephone. The records of the phone calls for Laura's phone were in the file, but Page 1 was missing.

- Database inquiries generated on October 30, 2000, in a separate folder, on John E. Brown, registered agent for John E. Brown Inc., 1301

Gervais Street, Columbia, SC. Brown was also affiliated with SKOWF, Inc., with affiliations in Pennsylvania and Florida. Also in the same folder were database inquiries on Kenneth C. Brown, the brother of John E. Brown. Kenneth also showed an affiliation with SKOWF, Inc., but Kenneth C. (known to his friends as KC) was listed as the chairman of AMPRO, the security agency formerly headed by John E. Brown.

Judge Davis told the truth. He thought it was Sgt. Collins who told him that John Brown was the initial suspect. Evidently someone thought he was enough of a suspect to run a nationwide database search on him and his brother, K.C. Brown. But someone stopped the investigation of the brothers.

Items missing from the file:

- There was no record of a statement from or interview with John E. Brown detailing his whereabouts on the morning of September 30, 2000 or his knowledge of Dr. Sunshine's death.
- There was no statement taken from Kenneth C. Brown giving his whereabouts on the morning of September 30, 2000.
- The photographs of the 1993 Lexus shown to Charles and me by Sgt. Collins were not in the file.

Sgt. Collins made one true statement to Judge Davis: Charles Outlaw would never go to trial. Better said, Charles Outlaw would never get a trial. Charles Outlaw never received justice.

As they say in the street, "You owe, and you know you owe." Somebody owed, and a debt was paid.

When I talked to the inmate at the women's prison, she told me that when Tshona and Charles were arrested some

"Jamaicans" cleaned out the apartment before the police got the search warrant. That sounded a bit bizarre, so I checked it out.

On March 8, 2004, I contacted the leasing agent for the apartments where Charles and Tshona lived. The leasing agent told me that she remembered "Jamaicans cleaning out the apartment" and that they must have had a key to do that because she did not give them a key. Charles had told me that when he got out of jail his clothes were missing from that apartment, as was the Acura that Tshona had been driving.

Later in the month, after Judge Davis' office denied having issued the search warrant for the apartment, I decided to contact Sgt. Collins directly. I called the District I headquarters and left a message with Captain Hancock. I was pleasantly surprised that Captain Hancock returned my call. I asked Captain Hancock about the search warrant for Charles' apartment and if he had any information about Sgt. Collins' involvement.

There was a meeting going on and Captain Hancock told me that Sgt. Collins was standing next to him, and handed the telephone to Sgt. Collins. Before Sgt. Collins got on the phone, Captain Hancock told me that he had heard that I had contacted the Solicitor's office asking questions. I assume he was talking about the Freedom of Information Requests. Word spread quickly between the agencies.

Why would someone at Barney Giese's office, the Solicitor, be talking to Captain Hancock about any inquiry I made to Mr. Giese's office?

I asked Sgt. Collins where the search warrant was issued. Sgt. Collins told me that the Lykesland Magistrate (Judge Davis) signed the warrant. I told Sgt. Collins that the clerk in Judge Davis's office denied the warrant came from that office.

On April 2, 2004, I called Judge Davis's office for the last time. I talked to Amber; she told me she looked on the logs and there was no record of the search warrant.

How did Sgt. Collins get a search warrant and it not be listed on the log of the magistrate's warrants?

Chapter Twenty-One

After Charles' heart attack in November 2003, Charles had a heart transplant in May 2004.

I was glad he lived, and we joked about the fact that if he died he would not be able to sue any of the persons or agencies that persecuted him.

There were many unanswered questions. I kept getting calls and snippets of information concerning the initial suspects and family members. I always checked with others for confirmation of things I would hear. It was hard to believe all I heard because the secrets were deeply buried.

Judge Davis did tell me that John Brown was the initial suspect, named by Sgt. Collins. That was rumor until I saw the database background check of John Brown and his brother in the file of the SC Department of Public Safety. If he was a suspect, where was the interview? Where was the investigation?

Who was the guy named Carlos who was pictured with Tshona in the Purple Passion strip club? Why did Forcina remove the photo from the hiding place where Charles put the photo?

Carlos was later identified as a driver for Johnny Brown while Johnny Brown was involved with Ampro Security. A former employee of Ampro told me that Carlos drove Johnny Brown, K.C. Brown, and an associate, Duane Everett, sometimes to Atlanta in a limousine.

Tshona had been telling her friends in prison that she was waiting for a big payday when she got out of prison. Who was going to pay her?

I met with Mark Sunshine, the son of Dr. Sunshine, and his attorney, in mid-2005. Mark remembered my name but my hair was quite shorter than it was when he saw me at the preliminary hearing. Mark told me he did not recognize me with my short hair and asked to see my driver's license. I wanted Mark to know the truth and he deserved to know that the truth had not been told. Mark called me back three times on the night I called him, which was the night before our meeting. He told me he was upset that he had been betrayed by the authorities he trusted. I had a draft of the case and agreed to meet with him on the following day. I gave him the draft. I told him that Laura Outlaw, and Charles as well, would be glad to speak with him to confirm anything he would want to know.

Mark told me that I was pointed out by Mr. Gasser in the courtroom, and Mark was told, "That is Jim Simms. Do not talk to him." Well, I guess they had their reasons.

I did not hear from Mark again after I gave him a rough draft of this book. I called him about four months later to see if he still wanted to talk to Laura or Charles about the case. Mark sounded like he was avoiding me. He told me he had no comment and could not talk about it. He sure changed his demeanor from the day I first talked to him.

The authorities attempted to keep me from witnesses in prison who had been in touch with Tshona. In mid-2006 I made contact with a former inmate who had been close to Tshona. That inmate knew my name. She told me that SLED had been investigating me, and that she was aware of the problem I had trying to interview the inmates. She told me to be very careful.

This woman told me that Tshona had told the inmates that the story about Johnny Brown being in the car was true, drugs and Jamaicans were involved, and it was not Charles' car that killed Dr. Sunshine. I asked her if K.C. Brown, Johnny's brother, was in the area. She immediately told me that Tshona said K.C. was in the back seat when Dr. Sunshine was struck by the car. According to this source Tshona said Johnny and K.C. got out of the car, removed Dr. Sunshine from underneath the vehicle, and left the scene. It was not clear if Tshona was in the car that hit Dr. Sunshine, witnessed the accident, or came upon the scene.

The reason Charles wanted a trial was because he wanted an attorney to stand up to the authorities and make them accountable. The information in this book is information which would have been presented in opening arguments, during the trial, and in closing arguments. Some of the allegations would be presented to witnesses during cross examination, and the witness could deny anything he or she wanted to deny. We would expect that, but we would be opening the door to the truth.

Chapter Twenty-Two

On February 2004, I accompanied Charles and Laura to Greenwood, South Carolina. Charles retained the services of Stephen Geoly to represent him against the SC Highway Patrol in the civil matter. Copies of documents were supplied to Mr. Geoly, and he acted very excited to take the case. He was paid five thousand dollars, which Laura had to borrow from family members.

A year and a half later, in September 2005, Mr. Geoly filed the Summons and Complaint without the knowledge of Charles, Laura, or me. There were no Interrogatories (questions to be answered) or Production Requests (a demand for copies of documents) attached to the Complaint. The Complaint was answered by the defense and the allegations were routinely denied. Mr. Geoly did not interview me after the initial meeting. (I did meet him once and watch him eat one evening in Columbia.) Charles told me many times that Mr. Geoly did not return telephone calls to Charles. I never received a return call from him. Faxes were sent to Mr. Geoly concerning the case and were ignored. In March 2006, the secretary in Mr. Geoly's office told me by telephone that she was going to conduct a deposition of witnesses and I was to be consulted with respect to who to depose, and questions to ask the witness. I never received another call from Geoly's office.

A hearing was supposed to be scheduled in the fall of 2006. Geoly's office called me on a Friday afternoon, asking if I would serve subpoenas to persons needing to be in court on the following Monday. That request was not possible to accomplish before the hearing date. Geoly allowed the case to be dismissed in January, 2007 and never told Charles. Charles could never get a return telephone call so he no way of knowing until I discovered the fact in November 2007. Charles had been betrayed by another attorney.

I continue to get calls about this case. Charles continued to hear things on the street, and all seemed quite consistent.

Laura and Charles would continue to talk to me. The case against the persons who did this to Charles had not concluded. Charles could never get any satisfaction from any attorneys to do the right thing for him. Even though Dennis Bolt, to his credit, did get the preliminary hearing for Charles, Dennis shied away from direct confrontation with the authorities. Even though Dennis was a friend and colleague, it was a surprise.

The big question was this: Why would the authorities go to the extremes they did to hide the identity of a black male passenger or any other passengers in the vehicle which killed Dr. Sunshine?

Chapter Twenty-Three

One Saturday morning in December of 2006 I called Laura just to talk and keep in touch. That morning she opened-up like she never had before. We talked about Charles' and Tshona's life in New York, and a visit Laura had with Tshona when Tshona was in jail. I had heard snippets of that information before, but while writing this book there were so many issues I just did not have the opportunity to have a long uninterrupted conversation with her. The following is what Laura told me.

Laura lived in Queens, New York and was a public-school teacher. Charles lived with her from time to time. Charles was a construction worker. Charles was a healthy young man and had his social life. His life would change after he met Tshona Gaymon.

Tshona Gaymon lived with her mother, Forcina, in an apartment in Manhattan on the Lower West Side. Tshona did not have a job; she was just out in the street pursuing men. According to Laura, Forcina was the same way.

Tshona showed up pregnant soon after she and Charles began seeing each other. Charles was not aware of all the other men who Tshona had been with, but Tshona charmed Charles and the baby was on the way. After Brandi was born Tshona continued to live with her mother and Charles lived with Laura. Charles also had an apartment of his own from time to time, but Laura's house was home base. Charles had a room/apartment in the basement of Laura's house.

Laura would not allow Tshona to move into Laura's house unless she and Charles were married. Laura had morals. Her husband had left her some time before for another woman, and she had raised their three children alone. She never divorced him. She did not condone what her husband did, and Laura was not going to condone the cohabitation of unmarried kids in her house.

Charles worked odd hours in construction in New York. If Charles kept the infant daughter it was usually at Laura's house. Charles moved back into Laura's house, and as Laura put it, she taught Charles how to care for the child.

Charles knew that at that time he was not married to Tshona and had no control over her. After Brandi was born, Tshona was back out "in the street" along with her mother Forcina.

As I said before, Forcina met Laura and told Laura about the relationship she had with Johnny Brown. Forcina had relatives in Columbia, and was said to have met Brown while out socializing in Columbia. Brown would supply Forcina with money and other "things" which were at his disposal. Forcina tried to get Laura to go out and find men like Forcina was doing. Forcina told Laura that Laura could put on makeup, do her nails, and go to the clubs and get any man she wanted. That was what Forcina was doing but Laura had been left by her husband and was raising three children; plus, Laura did not condone what Forcina was doing (and in front of Tshona).

There were times that Tshona would want to go out on the town. Laura knew that because Tshona would call Laura and ask Laura to keep the infant/toddler Brandi while Tshona went out. Many times, the child had not been fed. The only access to money that Tshona had was welfare money, and Tshona told Laura that she had already spent the money and not on the child.

According to Laura, Tshona was using men to finance her social life, just like her mother.

Laura told Tshona that anytime Tshona was going out and Forcina was not home, for Tshona to bring Brandi to Laura. In fact, Laura told Tshona that the child had better not be left with anyone that Laura did not know, and Laura was adamant about that. Tshona was so anxious one evening to go out with one of her girlfriends that Laura met Tshona in a subway station and Tshona passed the infant over the turnstile to Laura. These were the extremes Laura would go to in order to insure the child was protected.

Charles and Tshona eventually got married and came to South Carolina when Laura retired as a teacher. Forcina remained in New York but visited South Carolina. Upon arriving in South Carolina, Tshona became more familiar with her extended family in South Carolina, especially her aunt, Sandra Lambright, and Sandra's daughter, Mamchu Jeff.

When Charles was arrested for owning the car which killed Dr. Sunshine, Laura did not have the money to get him out of jail. As stated before, it was her cousin Happy who helped with the bail money. Happy not only told Laura that the word on the street was Johnny Brown and his brother K.C. were involved in the accident and/or had direct knowledge of it, but that Charles had better get out of the Richland County Jail before he was killed. Happy said to Laura that there were people in the jail who were supposed to kill Charles. Laura told me Charles said a health practitioner at the jail handed him a bunch of pills to take and Charles refused to take them. Laura then knew Happy was not bluffing.

Happy was told about the parking ticket from SC State University which was found in Charles' car when Charles bought the car. Happy told Laura that Carlos Parson, the driver for Johnny Brown, was the one who was down there on business for Johnny Brown. How would Happy know that? Happy knew dirt on everybody.

Laura worked at Dillard's department store in the late 1990s and Tshona worked alongside Laura. Laura said a security guard would stand near her from time to time and pat his baton into the palm of his hand, looking at Laura. Laura knew who he was but Laura did not have anything to fear. The security guard was K.C. Brown, the brother of Johnny Brown.

While working with Laura at Dillard's, Tshona would have a visitor who was familiar with not only Tshona but K.C. Brown. The visitor was Carlos Parson, Johnny Brown's driver. Carlos would show up carrying an umbrella, rain or shine. Tshona would disappear with Carlos into the store and Tshona would return in an altered state of mind. Laura told me that she reminded Tshona that she was from New York and she knew what was going on with Carlos and what he was delivering to Tshona. Tshona could not deny it.

It was Carlos' picture that Forcina took from Charles' apartment after the death of Dr. Sunshine.

Laura visited Tshona early on while Tshona was in jail in Richland County. Tshona told Laura that on the morning that Dr. Sunshine was killed, Tshona was driving south on Two Notch Road and saw a stopped black Lexus that looked exactly like Charles' black Lexus, which Tshona was driving. The other surprising thing was there were several notable black people in the car. Tshona told Laura that one of the occupants was a public official. Tshona said Carlos was driving the car. Carlos only drove for one person. A man's body was on the ground and a bicycle was on the ground.

Tshona recognized the people in the black Lexus. One of the persons told Tshona to get the hell out of there and to keep her mouth shut.

Tshona told Laura that she was scared.

Forcina had a number of siblings. Her brother, who was not identified before, was identified by Laura as Sgt. Gaymon, and was employed by SLED. John Brown's wife was employed by SLED. Chief Stewart refused to discuss this matter with me. The fact that I shared the results of the investigation with the Gaymon family did not insure that their connections to law enforcement (and elsewhere) were not getting the same information and getting a "heads up" on our defense of Charles Outlaw and the corruption which was to be exposed.

We might never know all the truth about all the persons involved in the death of Dr. Sunshine, but we do know the extent to which the authorities went in order to stymie the investigation, and insure that the cover-up, plus the killers' identities, would not be exposed in court. The Sunshine family were also subjected to this conspiracy by being led to believe the authorities, plus allowing the authorities to enable them to receive an insurance death benefit from Charles' insurance company when the vehicle was never proved to have struck Dr. Sunshine.

They certainly never expected me to expose it.

Afterword

The tragedy of Dr. Sunshine's death had many victims. My heartfelt sympathy goes to the family of Dr. Sunshine.

Most of us have lost loved ones as a result of an untimely death.

Charles Outlaw almost died as a result of the stress placed upon him during his ordeal. A healthy man his age does not routinely have to endure a heart transplant.

Charles was victimized by elected and appointed officials, people who knew what they were doing and no one stood up to protest. Others who were not directly involved could see the corruption and were too scared to say anything about it.

This story is not necessarily about who was in the car that killed Dr. Sunshine. I am sure that the "word on the street" will expose the persons responsible. The real story is about the depths that public officials plunged to protect the identity of persons who they probably did not know. The true character of these persons came shining through. These persons were elected or appointed to enforce laws, and to "protect and serve." They served their own self-interests and protected the criminals.

Many persons were involved in this travesty of "justice." Even though Sgt. Collins (who received a promotion and is now Lieutenant Collins) was at the forefront in this case, he was being directed and supervised by persons who allowed and encouraged this to happen. Even First Citizens Bank became a pawn in the agenda of the corruption.

The physical act of writing this book was not the difficult part of this project; the difficult part was reliving the anger and frustration at having to deal with the corruption, which included those who controlled my professional license. No one was accountable for this, and no one expected this to hit the light of day.

The Sunshine family was betrayed as was the trusting public of South Carolina.

I want parents to read this book and teach their children about the legal system in South Carolina, and the fact that this could happen to them. I want students to read this book and question their teachers, college professors, and law professors to find out how to make people accountable. I also want the law enforcement and legal community in South Carolina to read this book and have the courage to question each other.

J.B. Simms

www.ingramcontent.com/pod-product-compliance
Lightning Source LLC
Chambersburg PA
CBHW072103040426
42334CB00042B/2291